WITHDRAWN

DEMCO

THE ONE HOLY CATHOLIC
APOSTOLIC CHURCH

THE ONE HOLY CATHOLIC APOSTOLIC CHURCH

By
CONRAD BERGENDOFF

The Hoover Lectures
1953

AUGUSTANA BOOK CONCERN
ROCK ISLAND, ILLINOIS

THE ONE HOLY CATHOLIC APOSTOLIC CHURCH

⟦ PRINTED
IN U·S·A ⟧

AUGUSTANA BOOK CONCERN
Printers and Binders
ROCK ISLAND, ILLINOIS
1954

THE WILLIAM HENRY HOOVER LECTURESHIP ON CHRISTIAN UNITY

The Disciples Divinity House of the
University of Chicago

The William Henry Hoover Lectureship on Christian Unity was established by the Disciples Divinity House at the University of Chicago in 1945. Resources for the Lectureship are a Trust Fund established in the amount of Fifty Thousand Dollars some years prior to his death by Mr. W. H. Hoover, of North Canton, Ohio. The purpose of the Fund was designated as the promotion of Christian unity, a cause for which Mr. Hoover demonstrated a lifelong interest. Originally the Fund had been used for initiating publications, notably periodicals which have since become well established. With the successful launching of these enterprises it was decided that the cause of Christian unity could best be served by establishing at a major university center a lectureship on Christian unity, no such lectureship having yet come into existence. The Disciples Divinity House of the University of Chicago was asked to accept Mr. Hoover's Trust for the purposes of sponsoring a lectureship on Christian unity.

The intention of those establishing the Lectureship is that each lecturer shall be a distinguished Christian churchman of this or some other country, whose experience, research and knowledge eminently qualify him to discuss the problem of Christian unity and to make a positive contribution toward closer co-operation of the many Christian denominations and the ultimate unity of the church of Christ.

A series of lectures is normally given annually and published as the Hoover Lectures.   W. B. BLAKEMORE

To the Memory of

NATHAN SÖDERBLOM

whose vision of the unity of the Church in a
world torn asunder by international conflict
inspired for life those who knew him
these lectures are gratefully
dedicated

Foreword

To have the privilege of joining those who have already established a notable succession of lecturers on the Hoover Foundation is to be conscious of the responsibility owed to them, to the Disciples Divinity House and to William Henry Hoover in whose memory these lectures on Christian Unity were founded. No man may speak for the Church as a whole, nor even for that part of the Church he calls his own. But a man may witness to his faith in Christ in such a manner as to express also his conception of the Church through which he has come into the fellowship both of Christ and of other Christians. I seek in these pages to interpret the nature of the bond that holds Christians together.

The unity which can be predicated of the Church of Christ is a qualitative one, a unity consisting not in numbers but in properties which constitute the nature of the Church. The faith of the Church in unity cannot be considered apart from those qualities which are as essential to the Church as its oneness. No more simple or authentic profession of these characteristics can be found than in the statement we call the Nicene Creed. "One, holy, catholic, and apostolic Church" is the way the Church first defined its own character. Believing that this is still the most valid of definitions, I am proposing to consider the unity of the Church from the viewpoint of apostolicity, holiness, and catholicity. This will reveal, I believe, the meaning of unity. In brief, the unity of the Church in which the Christian confesses his faith is the unity of a Church which is holy, catholic, and apostolic.

CONRAD BERGENDOFF

Contents

I

The Apostolic Church

THE CHURCH of Christ is to be identified as the Church of the Apostles. This principle is as old and fundamental as the Church itself. It is, in fact, a sort of spinal column around which the structure of the Church has been formed. So central is its significance that the interpretation of the history of the Church is dependent upon it, and any hope of a united Church in the future must take it fully into account.

The criteria by which the Church is to be judged were forged in the heat and pressure of conflicting teachings, especially those dealing with Gnosticism. The definition of the true Church emerges from condemnation of false doctrine. From the very first the community of Christians was plagued by teachers who taught "the precepts of men" (Matt. 15:9). The Master himself had to contend with Pharisees and Sadducees. Paul had to admonish his co-worker Timothy to turn "away from the profane babblings and oppositions of the knowledge which is falsely so called" (1 Tim. 6:20). In the background of the whole New Testament is the false doctrine or false interpretations of the truth which the Church repudiated in its slowly-forming creed. Each phrase in that creed is aimed at a contrary doctrine then current.

Gnosticism was already widespread when the New Testament was being written. It was an ancient philosophy which saw in matter the principle of evil. Good was spiritual and salvation

1

consisted in the sloughing off of the material in order that the spiritual might be pure and free. God could not be credited with the creation of a world which is material and evil. So another creator must be found—a lower being than the true God, and to him the world owed its existence and character. Redemption must be thought of, too, as a spiritual process. Christ could not really become incarnate in a flesh which is evil. The divine world is set over against a material order from which the true man, the spiritual man, is to be saved.

Tantalizing as it is to pursue this old—and yet ever appearing—heresy, it is not here our purpose to try even to describe the many and varied forms which Gnosticism took. Here it is relevant only to ask, "How should Christians know that it was heresy?" There must be some standard by which doctrines could be tested and adjudged true or false. There must also be some accepted office to which Christians could turn for such a judgment. Both of these questions had found answers by the time of Irenaeus in the second half of the second century. The answers determined for centuries to come the character of the Church.

In his third book *Against Heresies,* Irenaeus explains that, "we have learned from none others the plan of our salvation, than from those through whom the Gospel has come down to us, which they did at one time proclaim in public, and, at a later period, by the will of God, handed down to us in the Scriptures, to be the ground and pillar of our faith. For it is unlawful to assert that they preached before they possessed 'perfect knowledge,' as some do even venture to say, boasting themselves as improvers of the apostles. For, after our Lord rose from the dead, (the apostles) were invested with power from on high when the Holy Spirit came down (upon them), were filled from all (His gifts), and had perfect knowledge: they departed to the ends of the earth, preaching the glad tidings of the good things (sent) from God to us, and proclaiming the peace of heaven to men, who indeed do all equally and individually possess the gospel of God. Matthew also issued a written gospel among the Hebrews in their own dialect, while Peter and Paul were preaching at Rome, and laying the foundations of the Church. After their departure, Mark, the disciple and interpreter of Peter, did also hand down to us in writing what had been preached by Peter. Luke also, the companion of Paul, recorded in a book the Gospel preached by him. Afterwards, John, the disciple of the Lord, who also had leaned upon His breast, did himself publish a Gospel during his residence at Ephesus in Asia. These have all declared to us that there is one God, Creator of heaven and earth, announced by the law and the prophets; and one Christ, the Son of God. If any one does not agree to these truths, he despises the companions of the Lord; nay more, he despises Christ Himself the Lord; yea, he despises the Father also, and stands self-condemned, resisting and opposing his own salvation, as is the case with all heretics."[1]

Noteworthy in this passage is the tracing both of the oral and the written tradition to the apostles, and the assertion of the 'perfect knowledge' possessed by them. This meant that the heretics could not rightly claim to hold another tradition or a more perfect understanding than the apostles held. The plan of salvation and the gospel are apostolic in their source. We have in another connection a succinct summary of the gospel which Irenaeus traced to the apostles, a sort of confession of faith in which the Church united and thus revealed its unity. Irenaeus writes, "The Church, though dispersed throughout the

whole world, even to the ends of the earth, has received from
the apostles and their disciples this faith: (She believes) in one
God, the Father Almighty, Maker of heaven, and earth, and
the sea, and all things that are in them; and in one Christ Jesus,
the Son of God, who became incarnate for our salvation; and in
the one Holy Spirit, who proclaimed through the prophets the
dispensations of God, and the advents, and the birth from a
virgin, and the passion, and the resurrection from the dead, and
the ascension into heaven in the flesh of the beloved Christ
Jesus, our Lord, and his (future) manifestation from heaven in
the glory of the Father 'to gather all things in one,' and to raise
up anew all flesh of the whole human race, in order that to
Christ Jesus, our Lord, and God, and Saviour, and King, according to the will of the invisible Father, 'every knee should bow,
of things in heaven, and things in earth, and things under the
earth, and that every tongue should confess' to Him, and that
He should execute just judgment towards all; that He may send
'spiritual wickednesses' and the angels who transgressed and became apostates, together with the ungodly, and unrighteous, and
wicked, and profane among men, into everlasting fire; but may,
in the exercise of His grace, confer immortality on the righteous,
and holy, and those who have kept His commandments, and
have persevered in His love, some from the beginning (of their
Christian course) and others from (the date) of their repentance, and may surround them with everlasting glory."[2]

This doctrine of the Church which had its source in the apostolic preaching has been communicated to succeeding generations by a succession of teachers. Irenaeus lived in the days of
the twelfth bishop of Rome. He is able to give us the names
of each of the successors of Peter (Book III, ch. 3) in Rome

which he says is worthy of pre-eminent authority. But he also claims, "We are in a position to reckon up those who were by the apostles instituted bishops in the churches, and (to demonstrate) the succession of these men in our own times." It is only because "it would be very tedious—to reckon up the successions of all the churches" that he confines himself to "the very great, the very ancient, and universally known Church founded and organized at Rome by the two most glorious apostles, Peter and Paul." In a later passage (Book IV, ch. 26) he specifically includes the presbyters in the succession. "Such presbyters," he says, "does the Church nourish, of whom also the prophet says, 'I will give thy rulers in peace, and thy bishops in righteousness.' Of whom also did the Lord declare, 'Who then shall be a faithful steward, good and wise, whom the Lord sets over His household, to give them their meat in due season? Blessed is that servant whom his Lord, when He cometh, shall find so doing.' Paul then, teaching us where one may find such, says, 'God hath p l a c e d in the Church, first, apostles; secondly, prophets; thirdly, teachers.' Where, therefore, the gifts of the Lord have been placed, there it behooves us to learn the truth, (namely,) from those who possess that succession of the Church which is from the apostles, and among whom exists that which is sound and blameless in conduct, as well as that which is unadulterated and incorrupt in speech."

Conduct is thus put on the same level as speech. The succession is not mechanical but consists in the conformity of the teacher and teaching with the apostolic norm. Irenaeus goes on to indicate the purpose of the succession, "for," he claims, "these also preserve this faith of ours in one God who created all things; and they increase that love (which we have) for the

Son of God, who accomplished such marvellous dispensations for our sake: and they expound the Scriptures to us without danger, neither blaspheming God, nor dishonoring the patriarchs, nor despising the prophets."

Not only, thus, are all teachings of the Church to be weighed and measured by the apostolic tradition, but the teachers of that tradition are themselves subject to it, be they presbyters or bishops. They do not determine the nature of the Church. At most, they can keep the Church in conformity to the apostolic witness. Only that Church is true whose doctrine and life are consistent with the apostolic tradition.

There can be little question that unity of faith in the early church meant a unity in the apostolic faith. In the face of many conflicting teachings there had to be a standard, a norm, a canon. This was true even while the apostles lived. Then they constituted an authority to which appeal could be made. As they passed from the scene their successors became the teachers, and the persecutions soon gave the bishops prior place as confessors of the truth. Ignatius could therefore lay the stress he did on the episcopal office. But it was the confession which glorified the office, not vice versa. While the bishop did judge the truth of doctrine he himself referred to a norm beyond himself. His function was to define truth as against heresy. To do this he fell back on the apostolic writings as the final authority. We may not be able to define in detail the place of the bishop in the first and second century, but we can be certain of the relationship of his authority to that of the apostles, and we can conclude that the Church came to a consciousness of what it was, in the degree that it related itself to the proclamation of the apostles. There is no evidence that the successors of the apostles ever felt that they had the right to define any new teaching beyond the Scriptural tradition. Their criticism of other teachers was that these introduced novelties. The most which the true leaders of the Church ever assumed was the right to judge whether any teaching was in conformity with the doctrine of the apostles. Only in this sense did they declare the faith of the Church. As little as the apostles were justified in adding to the teaching of Christ so little were the followers of the apostles entitled to introduce new doctrines. We might compare their function to that of the American Supreme Court which is not supposed to make law but to judge what is the law. It cannot be denied that in the process of the interpretation of the law, the law takes on new and even added meaning, but there is after all an acceptance of a standard, a charter, a constitution. The ministry of the Church had the function of repudiating false doctrine, not the making of doctrine. The Church became conscious of what its proclamation was to be as against what it was not to be.

I have cited Irenaeus as a representative of the period in which the early Church defined its own nature. Living in the latter half of the second century he is early enough to reveal the forces which became dominant in the Church and late enough to indicate in what direction the Church would move. By his time it was clear what teachings the Church would repudiate as heresies and by what standard teachings would be judged as true or heretical. The Church was definitely apostolic, and so described itself in the Niceno-Constantinopolitan creed of the fourth century. But already in the second century it was apparent that the unity of the Church would imply a conformity with the apostles' teachings. To Irenaeus certainly there

was no doubt that the unity of the Church consisted of its oneness in the faith of the apostles. "The Church," he observed,
"having received this preaching and this faith, although scattered throughout the whole world (and he goes on to mention
the churches in Germany, Spain, Gaul, the East, Egypt and
Libya) yet, as if occupying but one house, carefully preserves it.
She also believes these points just as if she had but one soul,
and one and the same heart, and she proclaims them, and
teaches them, and hands them down, with perfect harmony, as
if she possessed only one mouth."[3]

When in the sixteenth century the Church was shaken to its
very foundations and its outward unity was broken we find that
the issue in question was again the apostolic sanction. Almost
fifteen centuries had elapsed and the Church had become something undreamt of by Ignatius or Irenaeus. In the variety of
forms that marked the medieval church and in the novel prob-
lems which beset an hierarchy victorious over secular governments, it was natural that liturgy, creed, polity, all would develop
beyond the arrangements worked out by a small persecuted
church. But amid all change the principle of apostolicity had
lived on. It might run its course like an underground river
through the centuries, but occasionally it would assert itself before the eyes of all as in the apostolic fervor of the missionary
Boniface, the apostolic hope of Joachim of Flores, and the apostolic poverty of Francis of Assisi. And when, dammed up by
an accumulation of human ambitions and inventions the stream
forced itself over all of Europe separating everywhere the Church
into foe and friend, the appeal of Luther was to the criterion
by which the Church must be tested, namely, the apostolic Word.

One of the earliest and most effective of the polemical treatises of Luther was entitled "The Babylonian Captivity of the Church," written in 1520. Here was a trumpet call to reformation of the Church of Christ. That Church, Luther held, had lost its freedom, the charter of its existence, and was languishing in a captivity imposed by human tyranny. Striking at the most revered of the sacraments, the Mass, he admitted that changing it from a sacrifice to a sacrament would cause a revolution. He would be asked, "Will you not overturn the practice and teaching of all the churches and monasteries, by virtue of which they have flourished these many centuries? For the mass is the foundation of their anniversaries, intercessions, applications, communications, etc.—that is to say, of their fat income. I answer: This is the very thing that has constrained me to write of the captivity of the Church, for in this manner the adorable testament of God has been subjected to the bondage of a godless traffic, through the opinions and traditions of wicked men, who passing over the Word of God, have put forth the thoughts of their own hearts and misled the whole world."[4] Luther found the liberating word of God in the sacrament of baptism, in which man entered into God's rule over his life. "No one is bound to the traditions of the pope, nor does he need to give ear to him unless he teaches the gospel and Christ, and the pope should teach nothing but faith without any restrictions."[5] "So many orders, so many rites, so many sects, so many professions, exertions and works, in which Christians are engaged, until they lose sight of their baptism."[6] Discussing marriage and the multitudinous regulations of the Roman Church, Luther comes to the conclusion that "those things which have been delivered to us by God in the Sacred Scriptures must be sharply distinguished from those that have been invested by men in the Church, it matters not how eminent they be for saintliness and scholarship.''[7]

When he comes to the rite of ordination, he refuses to consider it a sacrament, and observes that "we ought to see to it that every article of faith of which we boast be certain, pure, and based on clear passages of Scripture." He finds no such basis for ordination, nor will he grant that the Church has power to institute a sacrament. "The Church has no power to make new divine promises, as some prate, who hold that what is decreed by the Church is of no less authority than what is decreed by God, since the Church is under the guidance of the Holy Spirit. But the Church owes its life to the word of promise through faith, and is nourished and preserved by this same word. That is to say, the promises of God make the Church, not the Church the promises of God. For the Word of God is incomparably superior to the Church, and in this Word the Church, being a creature, has nothing to decree, ordain, or make, but only to be decreed, ordained and made. —This one thing indeed the Church can do—it can distinguish the Word of God from the words of men. —Not that the Church, is, therefore, above the gospel; if that were true, she would also be above God, in Whom we believe because she proclaims that He is God. But, as Augustine elsewhere says, the truth itself lays hold on the soul and thus renders it able to judge most certainly of all things; but the truth it cannot judge, but is forced to say with unerring certainty that it is the truth."[8]

The Word of God is Luther's expression for the apostolic quality of the Church. As Irenaeus combined the oral and the written tradition in the apostolic books of the New Testament, so Luther identifies the Scriptures with the witness God has given man through Christ and the apostles. That witness is sure and clear, given to us in the writings of the apostles. Men have clouded or obscured that testimony by their own "opinions and traditions," they have "invented" ideas which contradict "those things which have been delivered to us." The Church has presumed to create doctrines beyond the Word. Every student of Luther knows how vehement the Reformer could be when he contrasted the inventions of man and the Word of God. No concept plays a larger role in his thinking than this "Word of God." It is to be understood in opposition to the mere words of man which in religion cannot bind any other man. It is remarkable that Luther speaks of the Word as liberating, making men free, whereas later generations have felt that the Scriptural testimony is a yoke and "liberalism" has meant emancipation from a biblical tradition. But Luther would still today, I think, claim that any human opinions or philosophies will turn out to be tyrannical, and that the freedom of the soul and mind depends on a promise of God.

The source of Luther's strength was in his deep-seated conviction that he was but "distinguishing the Word of God from the words of men." He would say of himself what he said of the Church, that he "is not therefore above the gospel." He goes back to a word of Augustine to explain his own experience. He cannot judge the truth, "but is forced to say with unerring certainty that it is the truth." What this truth is, is not his own idea—one more opinion among the many opinions of men, but his understanding of the Word of God as he heard it in the Holy Scriptures. Therein was revealed a criterion even for the Church. It was possible because of the revelation of the Word to judge the Church whether it was true or false. In that wherein the Church agreed with Scripture it was true. Where it departed from Scripture it could only claim human authority, and man was not bound by that.

Luther has not set himself as judge above the Church. He has set the apostolic gospel as the judge of the Church. The Roman Church had become autonomous and the Pope had made himself a vicar of Christ. Both Church and Pope are subjects, not sovereigns. Every Christian, clergy or lay, is bound by the same gospel and depends on the same Word of promise. Since it is the gospel given to us by the apostles, the Church is God's instrument for the proclamation of the apostolic witness. It ceases to be a Church when it departs from that witness. It is a church, and one church, in the degree that its testimony is consistent with the gospel received through the apostles.

In one respect there is a difference between Irenaeus' appeal to the apostolic tradition and Luther's. Both make the bearers of the tradition subordinate to the contents of the message. But Luther's historical situation explains his concern as to the character of the bearers. To Irenaeus the bishops and presbyters had distinguished themselves, often as martyrs, to conserve the tradition against persecutors and heretics. Luther's complaint was that the office bearers of the Church had proved themselves false in their trust. Hence the emphasis falls on the doctrine to be preserved. One feels that Luther's "Word of God" is a much more dynamic factor than the "tradition" of Irenaeus. It is the power back of the Scriptural Word, yet distinguishable in a sense from it. We might say that the Holy Spirit is a more living element in Luther's doctrine, and that the Spirit works also the power to judge the Church. Whereas Irenaeus is inclined to identify the Church and the apostolic tradition Luther has learned from a thousand years of history that the two are not altogether the same. The apostolic nature of the Church must include also the ability to judge the Church by a Word which is identifiable rather with the Scripture. So that Scripture becomes the judge of the Church even if the Church be the bearer of Scripture. In other words the Church must have within itself also the power of reforming itself. This it can do only by reference to something beyond and above itself—this is Luther's doctrine of the Word of God. We may say that Luther's achievement was to preserve the unifying element in the Church even at the expense of the division of the Church. For he found that man could never be the uniting force, whatever his philosophies or opinions might be. That which constituted the essence of the Church was a gift of God given men in the proclamation of the apostles. Word and sacrament made the Church—our faith in Word and sacrament gives us reverence for the Church. Our unity is in the testament of God of which the apostles were the witnesses.

No less emphatic than Luther, Calvin is the more systematic of the two in describing the character of the Church as apostolic. Book IV of the *Institutes* examines every form and activity of the Church. Everywhere it presupposes that the frame of the building must conform to the foundation on which it ultimately rests. "Let us lay down," Calvin urges, "this, then, as an undoubted axiom, that nothing ought to be admitted in the Church as the word of God, but what is contained first in the law and the prophets, and secondly in the writings of the apostles, and that there is no other method of teaching aright in the Church than according to the direction and standard of that word. Hence we conclude, also, that the apostles were allowed no more discretion than the prophets before them—namely, to expound the ancient Scripture, and to show that the things delivered in it were accomplished in Christ; but this they were only to do from the Lord, that is to say, under the guidance and dictation of the Spirit of Christ. For Christ limited their mission by this condition, when he ordered them to go and teach, not the fabrications of their own presumption, but whatsoever he had commanded them."[9]

Both the foremost of the apostles and the parish priest everywhere is thus regulated in the ministry by Christ's commission to all apostles: "Peter, who had been fully taught by his Master how far his office extended, represents nothing as left for himself or others, but to dispense the doctrine committed to them by God. 'If any man speaks,' says he, 'let him speak as the oracles of God;' that is, not with hesitation or uncertainty, like persons conscious of no sufficient authority, but with the noble confidence which becomes a servant of God furnished with his certain commission. What is this but rejecting all the inventions of the human mind, from whatever head they may proceed, in order that the pure word of God may be taught and learned in the Church of believers? What is this but removing all the decrees, or rather inventions of men, whatever be their station, that the ordinances of God may be observed? —This is the extent of the power with which the pastors of the Church, by whatever name they may be distinguished, ought to be invested—all in the word of God. Between the apostles and their successors, however, there is—this difference—that the apostles were the certain and authentic amanuenses of the Holy Spirit, and therefore their writings are to be received as the oracles of God; but succeeding ministers have no other office than to teach what is revealed and recorded in the Sacred Scriptures. We conclude, then, that it is not now left to faithful ministers to frame any new doctrine, but that it behooves them simply to adhere to the doctrine to which God has made all subject, without any exception."[10]

Luther could not be more explicit in limiting the Church to its original charter. Indeed, Calvin goes beyond Luther and gives to the apostolic tradition a certain inflexibility which was to affect the churches of the Calvinist persuasion for centuries to come. In three respects, especially, do we see the difference between these Reformers.

Calvin identifies the apostolic witness with the written word in such a way as to make the Scriptures a legal document. They are the "oracles of God" recorded by the apostles who were "the amanuenses of the Holy Spirit." The Word of God in Calvin has an objectivity unlike Luther's conception. Luther gives the impression of the flame that melts the metal, alive in the formative Word. Calvin bids us view the moulded form, fixed and unchanging. In both cases the Church is dependent on the Word which became flesh, but the result in each differs according to the character of the Word. Almost we might say, according to the tense. Is the Word one that *is* speaking—so that the Scriptures *now* glow with His voice? Or is the Word one that *was* spoken—so that the *record* is here before us?

A second difference lies in Calvin's greater emphasis on the Old Testament as a part of the Word. Prophets as well as apostles are the foundation of the Church. This is not to say that Luther thought any the less of the Old Testament. But his principle of the centrality of Christ made the horizon of Luther one which was dominated by the highest peak, whereas in Calvin's view of the revelation of God in Scripture Mt. Sinai was on a level closer to Mt. Calvary. For Luther the prophets were absorbed in the vision of the Crucified Christ. For Calvin the prophets were illuminated and given greater meaning by the light from Calvary.

A third, and fateful, difference is evident in the differing doctrines of the Church. Word and Sacrament testifying of the Son of God makes the Church for Luther. Calvin adds to his treatment of Word and sacrament "the order which it has been the Lord's will to appoint for the government of his Church,"[11] and places on this topic an emphasis unknown in Luther. So important does Calvin estimate it that he give a great part of Book IV to the sections on "the government—the power—the discipline of the Church." He considers that "the ministry of men, which God employs in his government of the Church, is the principal bond which holds believers together in one body" and that "whoever either aims to abolish or undervalue this order—and this species of government, attempts to disorganize the Church, or rather to subvert and destroy it altogether."[12]

I propose to discuss the consequences of Luther and Calvin's differing emphases for the field of church government under the rubric of the catholicity of the Church. We are here concerned with the apostolic basis of the Church. Both are clear that the church of Christ is not an institution of man's devices, but has its being in the tradition of the apostolic witness. The important difference lies in the interpretation of the extent of the apostolic sanction. Even the difference in regard to the objectivity of the Word was less important, for followers of Luther no less than those of Calvin tended to accept a verbal inspiration theory. Each applied this theory to what he decided was the apostolic teaching. But the significant difference related to the essential content of that doctrine. Luther concentrated on the Word of forgiveness in Christ, Calvin included the organization of the Church. As a matter of historical fact the Lutheran Church has in many places adopted a presbyterian form of government hardly unlike Calvin's plan. But the Lutheran has not felt that the question of discipline was a part of the apostolic injunction. The apostolic testimony was the gospel of grace in Jesus Christ—all else God left to human reason and Christian charity. Even the question of worship was an open one for the Lutherans, with the result that a great part of the traditional liturgy survived in Lutheran countries. The Calvinist tradition limited the forms of worship to such as had specific sanction in Scripture.[18] The Lutheran preserved what the Scripture did not forbid.

The Reformation reasserted the principle of apostolicity in its reconstruction of the Church. But it must be admitted that the limits of that doctrine were not agreed upon, and that the disunity of the churches of the Reformation results from a lack of agreement as to what God has revealed and what man may choose. The Reformers agreed that the Church of Rome had made the decisions of men of equal importance to the revelation of God, but the Reformers could not agree where the boundary line was to be drawn between that which was of God and that which was allowed man.

A significant example of this disagreement concerns the office of the ministry. Luther places little emphasis on the organization of the Church—it is enough for him that the Word is preached and the sacraments administered in a congregation where the Word judges even those who preach and lead in worship. Calvin claims that "in calling those who preside over churches by the appellations of bishops, elders, pastors, and ministers, without any distinction, I have followed the usage of the Scripture, which applies to all these terms to express the same meaning. For to all who discharge the ministry of the word, it gives the title of 'bishops'."[14] He contends that Scripture sanctions only the distinctions between pastors, teachers, and deacons.

Following the Reformation the Church divided into three great streams, each claiming apostolic origin for its course. The Church of Rome and the Orthodox Church maintained the ancient tradition of an apostolic succession. This tradition was explicitly defined at Lausanne, in 1927, when the representatives of the Orthodox Church in the Faith and Order Movement formulated this statement: "The Orthodox Church, regarding the ministry as instituted in the Church by Christ Himself, and as the body which by a special charisma is the organ through which the Church spreads its means of grace such as the sacraments, and believing that the ministry in its three-fold form of bishops, presbyters and deacons can only be based on the unbroken Apostolic Succession, regrets that it is unable to come, in regard to the ministry, into some measure of agreement with many of the churches represented at this conference."[15]

The second stream is represented by the presbyterian persuasion in which we would include both Lutheran and Reformed bodies, and the third by those churches which in general might be described as interpreting the doctrine of the universal priesthood of believers in such a manner as to eradicate any distinction between clergy and laity. However there are modifications of the presbyterian system which tend on the one hand toward the episcopal and on the other toward the congregational. The Anglican position seems to occupy a middle ground between the Orthodox and the presbyterian, as far as apostolic considerations are involved. Leonard Hodgson, explaining the doctrine of the Church of England to the Lund Conference of Faith and Order, in 1952, wrote, "Few Anglican theologians would now maintain that the threefold ministry of bishops, priests and deacons, as we have them today, can be directly traced back with their present differentialism of function, to apostolic times."[16] But Anglicans, he continues, look on episcopal organization as an indispensable means of communicating the gospel which unites "the Church of today to the Church of the Upper Room," and "regards its own maintenance of that succession as a treasure which it holds in trust for the Church universal, as one of the contributions which it has to bring into a reunited Christendom."[17] If this might be considered a course to the right of Calvin's presbyterianism, the Lutheran churches, with some exceptions—as in Sweden—would appear to the left. For the Lutherans view presbyterian government as effective though not divinely appointed, in somewhat the same way the Anglican looks on episcopacy, even though it be not divinely instituted in the measure held by the Orthodox.

Important as these variations may seem to be, it is even more important to stress that the primary thing is the apostolic message, and government is significant only as it helps perpetuate that message. Whether we feel that episcopacy or congregationalism or presbyterianism are apostolic or not in their origin, our interest in each is derived from its potency in communicating the one gospel revealed in the Scriptures. Even the deep-seated differences on this point are themselves an evidence of concern for the true and pure transmission of the message of the apostles.

An apostolic church is a church which is sent, a church with a mission. It is not a body which expresses itself, but which bears witness to something it has received. Granted, what it has received should transform the recipient, but the message is still more than what the messenger is. The essential message of the apostolic community is the gospel of the forgiving and creative love of God in Jesus Christ. This Word is the judge of even the Church. For unless there be a standard by which the Church can be judged the Church will make itself absolute. This is in effect what has happened in Christendom. But the Church is not absolute, it but witnesses to an absolute standard. That absolute is the divine Word of God by which the Church, its ministry and its mission, must be constantly judged. "In the beginning was the Word"—and until the end the apostolic Word will create the Christian community.

The ecumenical movement of the past thirty years has done much in bringing to light how large is the area of agreement among the churches on this criterion of apostolicity. There is no good reason why we should not take at face value the declaration of the delegates to the Faith and Order Conference at Edinburgh, in 1937, that "we all agree that the Christian Church is constituted by the eternal Word of God made man in Christ and is always vitalized by his Holy Spirit. On the other hand the divine task given to the Church is to proclaim and bear witness to this Word throughout the world by its preaching, its worship, and its whole life."[18] But there yet remains the sober task of defining this Word and distinguishing between the unchangeable elements of the Word and the changing elements—between the apostolic injunction, "Keep the great securities of your faith intact, by aid of the Holy Spirit that dwells within us" (2 Tim. 1:14 Moffatt's trans.) and the traditions which have their source in historical conditions and may change as circumstances change.

From very early times tradition has competed with the written scriptures as a source of authority in the Church. Naturally the oral tradition preceded the writing of the New Testament and determined its content. The question of precedence is, however, not significant since both the oral and written gospel were an expression of the faith of the Church as interpreted by the apostles. The expression of this faith was dependent on the Holy Spirit in the Church as much for either form. The later theory of the inspiration of the Scriptures is but another profession of the faith that the oral tradition was spiritually safe-guarded. Nor can there be a distinction admitted between the two on any important point. To base any doctrine on oral tradition as opposed to the written is but to follow in the footsteps of gnosticism, which claimed a superior knowledge derived from an unwritten tradition. Once started in that direction we are on the way to the disintegration of Christianity.

But while holding to the written Word as the sole arbiter of the faith of the Church, we do need to admit the role of tradition in secondary matters, such as organization, worship, the relation of ministry and laity, the attitude and practices of the churches with regard to the State. Indeed we will find that tradition not only deals with secondary aspects, but touches on the interpretation of the primary elements of the faith. The Greek Orthodox Church explicitly asserts the role of tradition in interpreting the doctrines of the faith, and it may be that all the churches should re-examine the nature of their respective traditions. Especially the churches which make the written Word the sole source of revelation need to discover how tradition has influenced their interpretation of the Word—what is considered essential, what is binding and what is conceded to freedom. The centrality of the doctrine of justification by faith in the Lutheran Church and the place of the doctrine of the ministry in the Episcopal and Presbyterian churches are themselves tradition-forming and traditional in these communions. There is no Church which has not been influenced by peculiar traditions, so that these traditions as well as considerations of doctrine have contributed to separation from other churches. Even some doctrines are the result of these traditions, rather than of biblical compulsion. So interwoven is biblical faith with post-biblical historical habits that one of the most urgent necessities of the ecumenical movement is to disentangle what is based on human tradition, what on the divine authority of the Word.

The apostolicity of the Church is limited to such doctrines as are clearly apostolic in their origin and application. Only in this realm can we hope for unity. No church can create apostolic doctrine, nor raise its own traditions to the level of apostolic authority. It may even be doubted that any one church can definitely establish what is apostolic. Both Peter and Paul had to submit to the Council of Jerusalem. A council of churches must have a part in the final resolution of differences which are caused by single churches claiming that only their's is the correct understanding of the divine Word.

From this point of view we look into the future seeking to discern some sign of greater unity among the churches as to what is the apostolic message. May we not believe that recent New Testament scholarship may help? For as we become more clear on what were the essentials of the message of the first century, applying the apostolic principle, we may be on safer ground in deciding what belongs to the kerygma, and what are the opinions of men—even sincere Christian men? Prof. Dodd for instance after careful analysis of the preaching of Paul and the other apostles, of Acts and the Gospels, comes to this conclusion, "In this survey of the apostolic preaching and its developments two facts have come into view: first, that within the New Testament there is an immense range of variety in the interpretation that is given to the kerygma; and, secondly, that in all such interpretation the essential elements of the original kerygma are steadily kept in view. —With all the diversity of the New Testament writings, they form a unity in their proclamation of the one Gospel.— The present task of New Testament criticism, as it seems to me, is the task of synthesis. Perhaps, however, 'synthesis' is not quite the right word, for it may imply the creation of unity out of originally diverse elements. But in the New Testament the unity is original."[19]

It is not true, therefore, that the disunity of the Church rests fundamentally on a lack of unity in the proclamation of the New Testament. There is one gospel, therefore there can be one message and one Church. But the nature of the unity of the kerygma has important consequences as to the nature of the unity of the Church. We may mention three of them.

One is the allowance of variation. There is a difference between Paul and John and Peter and Luke. While the differences provided opportunities for later diverging interpretations and disagreements the important fact is that all of the differences were within the apostolic fellowship and witness. Another interpretation did not necessarily mean another church, provided the essential message of Christ was ensured. There could be no omission of the fundamental historical facts or a change of their meaning, but one Gospel could add to another or the epistles of Paul could be quite different from those of John. The same freedom that characterized the early church should prevent divisions in the Church of our day. All too often members of the Church have been inclined to make tabernacles for themselves and to call these the Church of Christ. The very notion of freedom is more frequently met with in the pages of the New Testament than in some of the churches who claim themselves to be the heirs of the New Testament. The keynote of much denominationalism is not liberty, but conformity. May it be that the involvements of churches with secular government have had something to do with the spirit of legalism so often associated with the conformity demanded by churches? If we are to hope for greater unity in the Church we must pray for greater understanding of those who differ from us and greater allowance for such people. We are apt to let our likes and pride and ambition build the fences of our fellowship instead of letting Christ tell us who are the members of His Church. For it is after all His Church, to which He invites us—not our church to which we invite Him.

A second consequence of the unity of the gospel in the New Testament is this, that we may not make any but apostolic elements the points of separation from our brethren. There is no New Testament warrant for breaking the fellowship of Christians on matters of organization—no church can therefore set this up as a partition and demand any form as necessary for fellowship. A church that holds that all in communion with it must believe that the Pope is anti-Christ is adding something to the apostolic proclamation no less than a church which decrees that all of its members must believe in the assumption of the Virgin. When we demand that there must be unity of faith if there is to be fellowship in Christ, we must be willing to discuss what are the apostolic elements of faith on which agreement is necessary. All the churches have been guilty of too readily identifying themselves with the one church of the apostles—all of them have developed traits which they may like to keep as characteristic of themselves, but this is something else than saying that every one else must have these peculiarities. Our unity is in Christ, not in fellow Christians, and those who add to the terms of fellowship beyond what the New Testament demands are as guilty as they who take away from the words of prophecy—both are equally condemned in the final words of the Bible.

Thirdly, we may find that the road to unity will lead less through the barren wastes of controversy in which each finds fault with the other, and more directly through the fruitful fields of study in the elements of the apostolic kerygma. Much of modern preaching has little relationship to the gospel of Jesus Christ. And the farther the churches get from that gospel the farther they will find themselves apart. For we have no promise of any unity in speculations on panaceas for all the woes of mankind if our approach be on paths of sociology, economics, physics, psychiatry, or whatever be the latest fad. The promise of unity is in Christ. As we bring all these areas of the social studies and the natural sciences under His captivity we may learn that not even these can separate us from one another any more than from Him. But we are one because we have found

life in Christ. The only way to Him is through the kerygma of
apostles and evangelists and prophets. Turning toward Him
along with the company of the apostles we will find a unity we
will not hesitate to call that of the apostolic church.

NOTES

[1]Ante-Nicene Fathers, vol. I. pp. 414-15. (Christian Literature Publ. Co., 1886)
[2]Ibid. I:330-331.
[3]Ibid. I: 331.
[4]*Works of Martin Luther.* Holman Edition, vol. II. p. 209.
[5]Ibid. p. 234.
[6]Ibid. p. 236.
[7]Ibid. p. 261.
[8]Ibid. p. 274.
[9]*Institutes of the Christian Religion,* by John Calvin. 6 Am. Ed Phila. Trans by John Allen. Vol. II. p. 345.
[10]*Institutes,* II., 345-6.
[11]Ibid. p. 259.
[12]Ibid. p. 260-261.
[13]*The Worship of the English Puritans,* by Horton Davies, Dacre, London, 1948. This recent volume provides a detailed exposition of how this principle worked itself out in the Puritan congregations. "The real difference between the Lutheran and Calvinist reforms in worship may be summed up as follows: Luther will have what is not specifically condemned by the Scriptures; whilst Calvin will have only what is ordained by God in the Scriptures." p. 16.
[14]*Institutes,* II. p. 265-6.
[15]*The Second World Conference on Faith and Order,* Edinburgh, 1937. Ed. by Leonard Hodgson. p. 246. The Macmillan Company.
[16]*The Nature of the Church,* Ed. by R. Newton Flew. London, Student Christian Movement Press, 1952. p. 141.
[17]Ibid. p. 142-3.
[18]*The Second World Conference on Faith and Order.* p. 230.
[19]*The Apostolic Preaching,* by C. H. Dodd. Harper, 1936. p. 74.

II

The Holiness of the Church

AN ACUTE student of the Oxford Movement of a century ago claims that an inner tension marked the efforts of Newman and his friends, a tension between what he calls the static and the progressive elements. The static "was built up with Apostolic Succession as the cornerstone, and after the supposed ground-plan of the early Church." This was a more historic interest, conditioned by "aesthetic, intellectual, and traditional considerations." The progressive principle was religious and "its strongest driving force was the longing for holiness,"—this determined Newman's concept of the Church. "The true Elect are God's Saints —to say, that the true Church is the body of the elect, is only another expression for the idea that holiness is the most essential note of the Church." Yngve Brilioth believes that this longing for holiness explains "much of the power of attraction which Romanism has shown itself to have, particularly for the representatives of progressive New-Anglicanism. —to many of them Anglicanism was only a resting-place on the road that led from Evangelicalism to Rome. —it also makes it conceivable how this progressive New-Anglicanism would in the end endeavour gradually to remodel its own Church after the pattern of Rome: it has at least to some extent, nobler reasons than a single desire to imitate."[1]

This "holiness" movement of the 19th century was only one of a long series of similar endeavors appearing periodically in the Church and confirming Newman's estimate that "the idea of holiness is the most essential note of the Church." Long before the Church became conscious of its other attributes it knew itself to be a holy Church. The baptismal formula which underlies the creeds we call Apostolic and Nicene already in the first decades of the second century affirmed faith in unam sanctam— a holy Church.[2] In the New Testament the holy (οἱ ἅγιοι) are the Church. Paul addresses the church in Ephesus (Eph. 1:1) as "the· holy" in that place, and he identifies the "church of God which is at Corinth" with "them that are sanctified in Christ Jesus, called to be saints" (1 Cor. 1:2). The Christians at Colosse are appealed to as "God's elect, holy and beloved" (Col. 3:12).

New Testament scholars remind us that the concept of "the holy" derives from the Old, and in the New Testament usage we find echoes of priestly teachings concerning holiness.[3] The apostles knew of a holy people, a holy city, a holy temple. Holiness is not an ethical, but a religious term.[4] It has to do primarily with a man's standing before God, and since no man is good enough to appear before God, God must Himself do something to enable man to come into His presence. "The pure in heart shall see God" was the teaching of Jesus, but the purity he required was beyond man's ability to achieve. The righteousness man needed must itself be a gift of God—this was the truth Paul so clearly apprehended. Saints, therefore, are not those who present their virtues to God, but are they who through an inscrutable purpose of God are chosen by Him to receive the purity and righteousness which He requires. This is a gift apprehended only by faith. This faith justifies a man, makes him holy, set apart for God. He becomes a member of God's people, a branch of the holy vine, dwells in God's house, is a citizen of heaven. Through Christ we are participants in His body. The holy in brief belong to God. They are "his workmanship created in Christ Jesus for good works" (Eph. 2:10), "renewed in the spirit," new beings "that after God have been created in righteousness and holiness of truth" (Eph. 4:23-24).

It was natural that sincere Christians who had experienced the new life of holiness as a gift of Christ through the Church should come to expect that all who called themselves Christians show their faith in a holy life. Noteworthy is the shift of meaning which necessarily takes place in the use of the word "holy." Originally a saint, a holy person, is one who has experienced the new life in Christ. But inasmuch as it is a new life to which he is called, the life he leads is thought of as holy. First the Christian is purified in heart—then he leads a pure life. Only as experience reveals that not all Christians, nor all the life of any Christian, can be described as living in holiness, do we hear protests that the clean and the unclean shall be separated. The desire for holiness prompts the demand for a holy congregation.

Here we stand before one of the perpetual and universal phenomena in the Christian Church, which gives significance to the designation "holy" as applied to the Church. It is the phenomenon known in some periods as puritanism. It is an impulse in the very principle of reformation within the Church. It has given rise in some quarters to a distinction between a "visible" and an "invisible" Church. Within the Church this impulse has been more divisive than either the apostolic or the catholic principle. We cannot speak of the unity of the Church in any meaningful way without giving serious consideration to how Christians interpret the quality of holiness in the Holy Church.

It is impossible to understand the original Christian witness concerning holiness apart from the means by which one acquired this right relationship to God. Modern New Testament scholarship has discovered the place of worship in the early church. Protestant thought of the past two centuries has given the impression that becoming a Christian was a highly individualistic and intellectual process. A closer study of the sources reveals a Church which was above all else a congregation at worship, praising God for His deed in Christ, and seeking the gift of His Spirit, which was the Spirit of the Church, and in a unique sense the Holy Spirit. One entered the fellowship of this worshipping group through a specified course—instruction and baptism. Baptism was the beginning of this new life given by God, and was identified with membership in the congregation because the Church was the body of Christ. One lived the new life in the Church and was nourished therein. Above all the body of Christ revealed itself in the reception of the eucharist—the most intimate experience of living in Christ. "I have been crucified with Christ; and it is no longer I that live, but Christ liveth in me; and that life which I now live in the flesh I live in faith, the faith which is in the Son of God, who loved me and gave himself up for me" (Gal. 2:20). Participation in the holy Church was a participation in a fellowship which was instituted by baptism and meant an incorporation into the whole body of saints who lived in the eternal life of Jesus Christ. There is one interpretation of *communio sanctorum* which makes *sanctorum* refer to sacred things rather than holy people. Certainly the early Church thought of the Church as a communion of holy possessions—the sacraments were means by which the Holy Spirit made His a holy people.

Evidence abounds in the New Testament that holiness was not a characteristic of all the members of the apostolic church. The church at Corinth as described by Paul and the seven churches which are the subject of the first three chapters of the Book of Revelation seem startlingly like modern congregations. Yet as we read of these unworthy members we are aware of the concern of the writers. They deplore the actual conditions because of the lapse from the true standards of Christ's Church. "Remember therefore," the Church of Ephesus is warned, whence thou art fallen, and repent and do the first works; or else I come to thee, and will move thy candlestick out of its place, except thou repent" (Rev. 2:5). The early literature of the Church, the so-called *Apostolic Fathers,* has much to tell us of repentance and discipline. Though the standards of holiness were difficult the Church was conscious that its sincerity was tested by the lives of its members.

Yet from the first the holiness of the Church is not identified with the conduct of its members. There is a relationship to the Holy Spirit which seems even more fundamental, for ultimately the conduct of the Christian depends on this possession of, or by, the Spirit. In the letter to the Corinthians Paul passes quickly from the discussion of the behaviour of individuals to their reception of the Eucharist and to the matter of the gift of tongues. He rebukes the abuse of the latter but there is no doubt that he allows of a presence of the Spirit which cannot be rationally explained. And throughout the history of the Church we meet the same phenomenon again and again. "Quench not the Spirit" is an apostolic injunction to the Christians at Thessalonica set in a context of ethical admonitions (1 Thess. 5:19), and of a prayer that the God of peace would sanctify, or make them, holy. The Church has never found it easy to explain the significance of its sanctity, or holiness, but if we are serious about the unity of the Church we must come to agreement on the role of the Holy Spirit.

The first important schism in the Church concerned this very point. Toward the end of the second century, in Asia Minor, the Montanists challenged the accepted church leaders by appealing to a more direct operation of the Spirit. The details are not too clear. The protestants were orthodox in doctrine, and even Tertullian found it possible to join them. But they subordinated the bishops and teachers to the Spirit's influence. "For the first time," Bigg writes, "it was openly maintained by Christians that the Catholic Church was not holy and did not really believe in the teaching of the Spirit."[5] The controversy seems to have been the occasion for the first synods of which we have knowledge. Montanism was condemned, but the schismatics formed a separate church—the first conscious break in the unity of the Church. The separated church endured for centuries. We need not follow its history—"a harmless and maligned sect," Bigg calls its members, "whose main offense was that they were foolish enough to prefer a prophet to a bishop."[6] The important fact is to notice the relationship between direct contact with the Holy Spirit, a severe moral code, and a lay revolt against a crystallizing organization of the Church, along with a legalistic biblicism expressed in Tertullian's rule, "What is not expressly allowed in Scripture is forbidden."[7]

This is not the place to go into the story of monasticism, but it is necessary to remark that in its best forms this was an attempt to realize something of the holiness of the Church. Separation from a sinful world was an essential element in the concept of the holy. Men may have given this a geographical application, only to find that the world came with them into their caves and cells. But this well-nigh universal movement cannot be explained without admitting that somehow it gave expression to a valid desire to escape from the evil of the world into a holy place. It did not always lead to individual solitude. Sometimes groups, such as the Cathari in the earlier middle ages and the Brethren of the Common Life in the later, sought holiness in more normal relations of community life. But be it individually or in collective life the movement was a protest against a hardening of Christianity into formal behaviour and formal organization which seemed to leave little room for the Holy Spirit as a spontaneous and ever creative power. Something was missing in the "great" church, despite all its order and regularity. Certainly earnest Christians felt something missing in their own lives. The noblest of the protests in the medieval age was that of St. Francis. Unlike the Montanists and the Cathari and Albigenses, he was a devout son of the medieval Church, but his spirit was none the less revolutionary in that he sought to purify it from within. His biographer Sabatier has said of him that "the only weapon which he would use against the wicked was the holiness of a life so full of love as to enlighten and revive those about him, and compel them to love."[8] If we are to measure the unity of the Church in the first fifteen centuries we dare not magnify organization at the expense of holiness. To deny to the Montanists, or the Novatians, or the Donatists, or the Cathari, or the Lollards and Hussites, or the Albigenses, a place in the Church because of their refusal to obey the bishops or popes of the period, while they earnestly strove for the presence of the Spirit of God in their daily actions, is to construct an image of a Church which is far removed from the holy people of God as pictured in Scripture. This is not an endorsement of the gnostic elements in some of these sects. But it is a question worth considering whether the doctrinal aberrations of these communities were more serious in their effect upon the Church than the moral and "unholy" aberrations of the hierarchy. The history of the Church has largely been written by "court historians," and these have done less than justice to the earnest souls who have taken seriously the admonition "Ye shall be holy as I the Lord am holy." A Christendom which confesses its faith in a holy Church must have a concept of unity which satisfies those who believe in a Holy Spirit.

The importance of this fact becomes apparent with the Reformation. For now on a grand scale the Church divided on the question of what constitutes holiness, and divided in several directions. From one point of view the doctrine of justification by faith is a doctrine of the nature of holiness. Can the Church make a man holy? When Luther concluded that man is justified only by faith he denied the power of the Church or its ministry or its sacraments to make a man holy. Only the Holy Spirit could do that and man's faith was a requisite. The righteousness of God was a gift to man, not to be earned by any man's accomplishments. The holiness of the Church consisted in the Holy Word and Holy Sacraments which it had to proclaim and administer to mankind. The presence of Christ the Word alone makes the Church holy, faith in the Word makes the Christian holy. In his treatise "On the Councils and Churches" 1539, Luther thus interprets this article of the Creed:

"If these words had been used in the Creed: 'I believe that there is a holy Christian people,' it would have been easy to avoid all the misery that has come in with this blind, obscure word 'church.' For Christian holiness, or holiness of universal Christendom is that which comes when the Holy Spirit gives people faith in Christ, according to Acts XV, that is He makes heart, soul, body, works and manner of life new and writes God's commandments, not in tables of stone, but on hearts of flesh according to II Cor. 3." He goes on to claim that the Christian, holy people is to be known by its possession of the Word, the sacraments, the office of the keys, the ministry, and by its exercise of prayer, praise, and thanksgiving and its bearing of the Cross.[9]

The stand of Luther differentiates him from both the Roman Church and the group of churches at that time designated loosely as Anabaptist. Over against Rome he contended for a personal decision of faith which undermined the Roman sacramental theory. Word and sacrament were no less objective realities to Luther than to Roman theology, but he could think of neither apart from Christ and faith—Christ being active in the preaching of the Word and present in the sacraments. Rome, on the other hand, thought of grace in terms of infusion and application and of the sacraments as in themselves effective. Canon 8 of the Seventh Session of Trent decreed that "if any one saith, that by the said sacraments of the New Law grace is not conferred through the act performed (ex opere operato non conferri gratiam), but that faith alone in the divine promises suffices for the obtaining of grace, let him be anathema." On the performing of the acts called sacramental Rome built a whole system which made for the holiness of its members. The Protestant reformation went back to a more immediate communication between Christ and the Christian through which the believer might obtain holiness.

Yet Luther would not go as far as the Anabaptists, who were inclined to eliminate not only the Roman sacramental system but also the Lutheran conception of the ministry. Luther held to a ministry of Word and Sacrament as essential to the existence of the Church,[10] and practically made of it an order or estate, which indeed it became in the orthodox conception of society composed of three estates. The Anabaptist abolished the ministry altogether except as it was inherent in the congregation. The term Anabaptist is not exact, and those who were given the name received scant justice in the time of the Reformation.[11] Only more recently, and in America, are we beginning to see the significance of this group of dissenters who were not large or successful enough to gain recognition either in their time or later. But they held to a theory of the Church which had had an underground existence since the beginning and which, since the Reformation, has influenced wide areas of Christendom. I quote a characterization of them by Max Goebel to indicate their idea of a church and its holiness. "The essential and distinguishing characteristic of this group is its insistence upon the actual personal conversion and regeneration of every Christian through the Holy Spirit, upon full freedom of conscience and religion, upon separation of spiritual and worldly things, of Church and State, and upon the establishment of a true holy Christian Church of the reborn—which by means of Christian discipline and the ban would exclude everything worldly and sinful and on the other hand would carry out the Christian principles of true brotherly love by means of a sharing of (spiritual and material) goods and through a weaponless and revengeless life. They aimed with special emphasis at carrying out and realizing the Christian doctrine and faith in the heart and life of every true Christian in the whole Christian Church, and therefore at the bringing together of all true regenerated believers out of the great degenerate church into a new holy church. —That which the Reformation actually originally intended they aimed to accomplish."[12]

One thinks immediately of "the gathered church" of England and America of the following century, and the program of the Pilgrims and the Congregationalists is very similar, except in its relations to the state. But in all these churches, which followed neither Rome nor Wittenberg nor Geneva, there was a desire for a holy church, where the tares had been separated from the wheat and the members of the Church lived holy lives. The novelty lay in the attempt to construct a church on these principles. The longing for a purification of the Church was not new. What the followers of Conrad Grebel tried to do in the Swiss and Dutch Mennonite churches was not essentially different from what two other great reformers purposed as they hoped to purify the Church from within. All of them witness to a common faith in the need of the Church to be holy.

One was Spener. Depressed by the condition of the Lutheran churches in Germany after the Thirty-Years' War and the frightful moral decline of a people which still considered itself orthodox, Spener analyzed the weakness of both clergy and people, proposing reforms in home, church, university. He appealed to Luther's doctrine of the priesthood of all believers hoping to arouse the laity to a sense of their individual responsibility instead of leaving all religious concerns to a ministry which itself

was slack in life but arrogant in attitude. Earnestly he urged
that the people must be taught the lasting principle "that it is
absolutely not enough to associate Christianity with a certain
kind of knowledge," but they must be made to see that "Christianity consists much more in the daily practice."[13] Referring to
a series of New Testament passages, he reminded his readers how
often the Saviour described love as the mark of His disciples,
and he repeated the story of Jerome about the aged St. John
who so often admonished his followers to love one another
that they finally asked him why this constant maxim, to which
he replied, "Such was the Master's command—if that be obeyed,
all is well." Spener adds that the whole life of the Christian and
the fulfillment of the divine commandment consists in love, and
that if such a love existed among Christians and toward all—
"brotherly and universal love must accompany each other"—
practically everything which he was striving for in the Church
would be realized.[14]

The founder of Pietism yielded not an inch in his doctrinal adherence to the confessions of his church, but he added
a dimension which had been crowded out in the bitter contro-
versies following the Reformation. The witness of a loving life
was of equal importance to him with doctrinal defence of the
truth, and followers such as Francke and Zinzendorf put into
practice his proposal for a reformation within the Church.
Grebel and Spener would never have agreed on the constitution
of the congregation, but both of them sought the building up
of the kingdom through purified and dedicated lives on the
part of those who called Christ their Saviour and Master. It is
one of the remarkable events of church history that German

Pietism and English Puritanism should later interact on each other and help purify and fructify the whole of Protestantism.

Of no less stature was John Wesley. Himself a priest of the Anglican Church, and always sympathetic with both the worship and the three-fold ministry of that Church, he sought to promote its purity from within. It is well known that Wesley intended his movement to be a *Church movement,*[15] but he did not consider loyalty either to the organization or the regulations of the Church of England as supreme, submitting himself to what he believed a higher purpose, namely, "to promote, so far as I am able, vital, practical religion; and by the grace of God to beget, preserve and increase the life of God in the souls of men."[16] Circumstances forced him to organize a separate church, but it was in the hope of influencing the wider Church. "Always," says Lee, "he maintained his passion for holiness, which demanded of him the constant imitation of Christ, which led him not only to form religious societies, but to use constantly the means of grace. But orientated with this was a conscious religious experience, embracing trust and insight and the fruits of the Spirit, love, joy, and peace."[17]

The British Methodist Conference of 1937 has recorded how strong still is the determination of Methodism to stress the individual experience of its members. The task of Methodism "was and is" it declared, " 'to spread Scriptural Holiness through the land.' The influence of one human personality on others is the chief means used by God for propagating the truth by which the Church lives. Most men are won to Christian faith, or confirmed in Christian conviction, by the beauty of Christian character, the attraction of holiness embodied in personal form. Behind each believer of today there stretches a long chain, each

link a Christian man or woman—a succession of believers—
(with) no distinction between laymen and ministers, men and
women. Indeed, all Christians may be priests in this holy office."[18]

One difference between Spener and Wesley is an index of
two different attitudes toward the world outside of the Church.
Will a holy Church affect society as a whole, and how? There
is a difference here between German and British reformers
which may have many non-doctrinal causes. Some would call it
the difference between optimism and pessimism, or find the root
in historical, psychological, sociological factors. Wesley was only
one of many British spokesmen who talked as if the holiness of
the Church might sanctify all life. William Law, whose *Serious
Call to a Devout and Holy Life* (1728) had immense influence,
was a good Anglican, yet could write such Wesleyan aspirations
as these, "This, and this alone, is Christianity; an universal holiness in every part of life, a heavenly wisdom in all our actions,
not conforming to the spirit and temper of the world, but turning all worldly enjoyments into means of piety and devotion to
God,"[19] and "It is the very end of Christianity to redeem all
orders of men into one holy society, that rich and poor, high
and low, masters and servants, may in one and the same spirit
of piety become 'a chosen generation, a royal priesthood, an holy
nation, a peculiar people; that are to show forth the praises of
Him who hath called them out of darkness, into His marvellous light.' "[20]

Certainly the Germans of the Spener tradition would desire a
Christianization of the world, but there is lacking in Lutheranism the expression of the hope that this can ever be. It may
not be unfair to say that British and American Christianity has

been more apt to think of a holy people, a new Israel, and the German and Scandinavian, of a holy remnant. The Lutheran preoccupation with confessional statements, which the Anglican and the Free Churches find hard to understand, is really an attempt to distinguish the Church from what is not the Church, to keep the boundaries clear between the world and the Church. The more confident and enthusiastic Anglican, Presbyterian, Congregational and Baptist churches have been more interested in crossing the boundary and bringing the influence of the gospel to those outside[21] Generalizations are dangerous and futile and I make these with reservations, but there is a difference between these branches of Christendom in regard to the holiness of the Church which calls for much closer study than has hitherto been given to it. No unity of the Church can be gained which fails to take into account this deep-seated difference in respect to the separatedness of the Church from the world.

A very different emphasis is found in the Greek Church. A modern archbishop of Greece, Chrysostom, in a contribution to the Lausanne Conference, stressed the fact that "the Church is made holy by the Holy Spirit—not that the members of the Church individually are all holy; it is the Church that is holy, and this does not mean that it has none but holy members. —the holiness of her members is the aim which the Church aspires to reach through the means afforded to her. The inclusion of members who are not holy does not destroy the holiness of the Church, nor prevent it from making spiritual progress. A tree may have some withered branches, and yet go on growing, as long as its roots are strong and healthy. Deriving her sanctity from her Head, the Church ever seeks the betterment of her weak members, and only casts out from her fellowship those who cannot be made better."[22] Holiness here is associated with holy things: the holy sacraments, a holy ministry, a holy liturgy, a holy faith. The roots, rather than the fruits, are proof of the holy Church.[23]

From whatever period or whatever land we take our examples, always we find an insistence on holiness as a quality of the Church. It is not enough to say, with Bigg[24] that all these manifestations of a longing for a holy life derive from the mysticism which time and again breaks out in the Church. They are a profession of faith in a holy God whose presence is known to us only by a Holy Spirit which through holy means would give us the gift of holiness. Repeatedly the Scriptures have promised the people of God that they shall see God and they confess that they have seen Him in Jesus Christ and shall see Him face to face. The vision of God demands holiness. The Church has variously interpreted that holiness. At best it sees here only in part. But wherever that longing for holiness has existed Christ has not been far away, for it is his Church which inspires it. Wherever men confess faith in the Church they describe it as a holy Church, and none can say how many or who they are who have united in this confession.

We shall find that the disunity of the Church is bound up with the difficulty of resolving a tension which has always existed between the quality of holiness and that of catholicity. The catholic spirit aims at fullness which implies inclusiveness. The whole must be achieved in a way that omits no integral part. The spirit of holiness operates so as to exclude. We have observed that in its root meaning holiness expresses a separation, by which the holy things and the holy people are differentiated from the world. Not everything belongs in the whole. Christianity witnesses basically to a dualism. Whereas Oriental faiths are fundamentally monistic and end in an All which absorbs everything, Christianity moves toward a final judgment which divides between sheep and goats, good and bad, tares and wheat. It is on this account misleading to identify the Christian idea of holiness with the general concept of mysticism. There is in Christianity an ethical aspect of holiness unknown in other religions. The people of God are to go out from the world—the principle of their vocation is a mystery known only to God. That is one side, but only one side. The other is that those who are called are called to an obedience of the will of God. Luther stressed the former truth—we are chosen through no merit of our own, we are justified only by grace. Calvin stressed the other truth—there is an obedience of faith, which issues in a godly life. Luther stands closer to the Roman and the Greek churches in his emphasis on the Church as a steward of holy things, possessing the means of holiness. Calvin is more closely related to all the groups which judge the Church by its fruits and emphasize the kind of life the means of grace should produce. In the former churches we find a fully developed doctrine of the ministry, in the latter more attention is paid to the laity. There is agreement that the Christian life is a holy life but no agreement as to where the boundary should lie between the holy and the profane.

This lack of agreement has affected not only the various positions of Christians on the matter of the individual's sanctification, and of the policies of churches as to internal discipline. It has caused wide differences on the point of the relationship of church and education, church and culture, church and state. Does the Church of Christ have a mission to society at large or is its function restricted to the separated flock? If congregations are to be composed only of those who are conscious of their separation from the world, shall the Church withhold the sacraments from those who may be on a borderline and where shall that line be drawn? These are questions which have been differently answered in different parts of Christendom, under circumstances of place and time peculiar to those parts. Those answers today underlie some of the divisions of the Church and are historical heritages not to be measured by some yardstick of holiness which has little relevance to social groups and traditional societies.

In general the so-called state churches have assumed a role of bringing the gospel to bear on all aspects of national life which the free churches have, in their origin, criticized. Yet, curiously, these free churches have often advanced to a social interest and activity which prohibits us from making the judgment that the free churches have been interested only in individual holiness. But there seems to be a deeply seated difference between the two as to whether society can be purified from within or from without, that is, does the church which has no government connection stand in a better position to criticize and propose changes than the church which stands in economic dependence on the state? Even those churches which have traditionally stood most aloof from involvement in national life have in our generation shown a remarkable interest in relief of war-stricken countries and in concern for international peace. Almost all Protestant churches and the Roman Church through the Vatican have in our century seen an obligation of the Church to social questions which is unprecedented in church history. We can on longer draw the line which former generations drew between churches interested only in a world to come and those intent on influencing the present age. The line of cleavage seems rather to run along the question of *how* Christians can best witness to the existence of a holy kingdom of God here and hereafter. How shall the witnessing church maintain its identity over against those who are not Christian? How shall the salt preserve its savor as it loses itself in an undifferentiated society?

Much can be said for the effectiveness of both the state and the free churches. The former include the Orthodox, and the Anglican and Lutheran communions and it is not merely a coincidence that they are also known as the liturgical churches. For the liturgy is corporate worship and embodies in itself elements in the education of a society which has had much to do with the life of whole peoples. These are the churches too which in the West have traditionally been interested in education, confessing thereby a belief in the application of the gospel to all the arts and sciences of man's knowledge. In acknowledging the weaknesses of these massive churches, we should not forget their immense contributions to social stability, national morality, and the character of peoples.[25] They have fortified themselves in a way by a doctrine of the ministry which has thrown the weight of the demands for holiness on a "holy order," whose function is to safeguard the holy treasures of the faith. The free churches have pointed out the impossibility of securing complete sanctification of all who thus are given the name of Christian. They have found occasion to question the holiness even of the official ministry. They have given examples of rigorous selection of members of their own group, and accomplished miracles in their own effective action in government, in evangelism, and purity of social life. But there has always been the problem of the second and third generations—here the free church has been no more successful than the folk-churches. Holiness is not inherited. Continuity of a ministry can be achieved and so the identity of a denomination secured. But there is no succession of holiness. "The Holy Spirit bloweth where it listeth" and defies a definition which restricts Him to any one human ordering. A holy church is no more possible than a holy society[26] if the criterion be the holiness of all its members. And if the holiness of the members is not the criterion but the presence of the Spirit in Word and Sacrament, then the members have nothing of which to boast. Theirs is the duty to pray that He may come to them, and to meet Him where He has promised He would be. They cannot even demand that He come because they have Word and Sacrament—there is no way in which they can control or command Him.[27] It is not they who have made a contract with Him and which they can enforce. It is He who has given them a promise, that all may be of grace. If we take Him at His word, we may believe He will not fail us. On such a foundation only rests our faith in holiness. And lest we make a distinction between justification and sanctification, so as to give God the praise for the first and reserve some honor for ourselves in the latter, let us remember the sentence from the Edinburgh Report, "Whatever our growth in holiness may be, our fellowship with God is *always* based upon God's forgiving grace."[28]

When we try to locate the holiness of the one Church of Christ we must move beyond all churches (not outside of them) to Him of whom it is written that, "there is no searching of His understanding" (Isa. 40:28) and "His ways are past tracing out" (Rom. 11:33). The Creator of the ends of the earth and the Lord of history is also the maker of every individual and every community which can be called holy. He calls both the Old and the New Israel out of an environment of sin and gives them of His own holy nature. Luther does not hesitate to speak of the Church as a mother "that bears every Christian," but as we read on in the context of his explanation of the Third Article of the Creed, we discover that it is the Holy Spirit "who makes, calls and gathers the Christian Church, without which no one can come to Christ the Lord." This Christian Church Luther defines in a way that includes everyone who has been sanctified, and "sancification is nothing else but bringing us to Christ to receive this good to which we of ourselves could not attain." I know of no more ecumenical description of the holy Church than these words of his: "I believe that there is upon earth a holy assembly and congregation of pure saints, under one head, even Christ, called together by the Holy Ghost in one faith, one mind and understanding, with manifold gifts, yet one in love, without sects or schisms. And I also am a part and a member of the same, a participant and joint owner of all the good it possesses, brought to it and incorporated into it by the Holy Ghost, in that I have heard and continue to hear the Word of God, which is the means of entrance. —Until the last day the Holy Ghost abides with the holy congregation or Christian people. By means of this congregation He brings us to Christ and teaches and preaches to us the Word, whereby He works and promotes sanctification, causing (this community) daily to grow and become strong in the faith and fruits of the Spirit, which He produces." *(The Large Catechism)*

The holiness which unites the Church is not to be found in the members of the Church. Despite all the varying emphases on the quality of holiness to be found in the record of the churches it is clear that holy people cannot create one people. Agreement lies not in them but in their testimony that "One is holy" and all holiness is derived from Him. Bishop Aulen, a leader in ecumenical discussions has written, "The unity of the Church cannot be built upon our own sanctity, nor upon a flawless doctrine. —We cannot build upon our own endeavours and performances, only upon the fact that 'we have among us the Word and the Sacraments that sanctify us.' —these constitutive factors of the Church stand above doctrine—and the unity of the Church is deeper than any doctrinal uniformity. Christ works through the Word and the Sacraments in spite of human misunderstandings. To consider a doctrinal uniformity as a foundation of the unity of the Church would be also to build it upon a human achievement, in this case a theological one. The Kerygma, the Gospel, comes before every human interpretation."[29]

Our study reveals probably all too clearly that the divisions within the Church in regard to the interpretation of holiness follow no doctrinal pattern. The prayer "Make me clean" arises from every part of the Church, and the longing for holiness cuts across all denominational lines, be they those of free church, state church, liturgical or non-conformist. Here is an evidence for the unity of the Church which baffles those who would seek for more tangible and controllable forms of oneness. But the very newness of the Christian life which reveals its holiness threatens the bottles containing the new wine, and no standard form of bottle creates the wine to fill it. Any unity of the Church must provide for an activity of the Spirit which is unpredictable, inexplicable, and immeasurable. Authorities in the Church have too often been ready to quench the Spirit where it has not yielded to ecclesiastical analysis. A new birth of understanding, charity and patience will be necessary if a holy house of God is to be built in which all the children of grace are to find a habitation.

NOTES

[1] *The Anglican Revival*, by Yngve Brilioth, Longmans, Green & Co., 1933. pp. 127-8, p. 260.

[2] *Die Theologie Des Neuen Testaments*, Ethelbert Stauffer. 4th Ed. Gütersloh, 1948. p. 228. Harnack thinks the article on "the holy Church" goes back to the middle of the second century when the baptismal formula was being formed and that its presence in Marcion's creed implies it was already a rubric in the Old Roman symbol. "Das Alter des Gliedes 'Heilige Kirche' im Symbol," pp. 171-3, *Aus Schrift und Geschichte, Theologische Abhandlungen Adolf Schlatter dargebracht*. Stuttgart, 1922.

[3] *Hágios* in *Theologisches Wörterbuch zum Neuen Testament*, von Gerhard Kittel, Stuttgart, 1949., I. pp. 87ff.

[4] "bei der Heiligkeit immer von der zuständlichen Sittlichkeit der 'Unschuld,' nicht vom sittlichen Handeln die Rede ist. Die zuständliche Sittlichkeit hängt aber mit der Kultfähigkeit aufs engste zusammen. Man darf deshalb Hagiotés und Hagioi niemals mit 'Sittlichkeit' und 'sittlich' übersetzen, da sonst das Element des *religiosun* verloren geht." Ibid. p. 110.

[5] *The Origins of Christianity*, Charles Bigg (Oxford University Press, 1909). p. 187.

[6] Ibid. p. 189.

[7] Ibid. p. 190-1.

[8] *Life of St. Francis of* Assisi, Paul Sabatier. Scribner, 1924. pp. 45-6.

[9] *Works of Martin Luther*, Holman Ed. Vol. V. pp. 265 ff.

[10] A recent work, *Creator Spiritus*, by R. Prenter, Muhlenberg, 1953, gives a clear picture of Luther's position, both before and after his controversy with the "Enthusiasts."

[11] "Die Täufer sind nicht nur Stiefkinder der Reformation, sondern auch der Forschung gewesen" (The Baptists are step-children not only of the Reformation but of research)—foreword of *Quellen zur Geschichte der Wiedertäufer I* (Leipzig, 1930). Quoted by Gunnar Westin in "Döparrörelsen som forsknings-object" in *Uppsala Univ. Årsskrift*, 1952, p. 52. Westin describes how recent research is discovering a new picture of the Anabaptists, distinguishing between the "Enthusiasts" or "Spiritualists" who were individualists, and the congregation-forming Baptists who carried farther than Zwingli the interpretation of a church based entirely on Scriptures. The latter group is quite a different branch of the Anabaptists (a term too broad to have clear meaning) than are the followers of Thomas Muntzer. Conrad Grebel and Menno Simons are founders of Brethren and Mennonite churches—the "Spiritualists" left no churches.

[12] Quoted in *Conrad Grebel* by Harold S. Bender. Mennonite Publishing House, Herald Press, Goshen, 1950. p. 210.

[13] *Pia Desideria* (1675) Philipp Jacob Spener. Leipzig, 1841. p. 75.

[14] Ibid. p. 76.

[15] cf. *John Wesley and Modern Religion*, Umphrey Lee. Abingdon Press, Nashville, 1926. p. 246. Lee calls attention to the Religious Societies of the time. The St. Giles' Cripplegate society had in its rules "that the Sole design of this Society, being to promote Real holiness of heart and life." p. 24.

[16] Quoted by Lee, p. 261, from Wesley's *Letters*, vol. 3. p. 192.

[17] Lee, op. cit. p. 105.

[18]*The Nature of the Church.* Ed. by N. Flew. Student Christian Movement Press, London, 1952. p. 207.

[19]*A Serious Call to a Devout and Holy Life,* by William Law. E. P. Dutton & Co. Everyman Edition. p. 113.

[20]Ibid. p. 277.

[21]Such a statement as that of Kagawa would hardly come from a Lutheran source, "A Christian society, and nothing less, is the goal of the Kingdom of God Movement. Our aim is the thoroughgoing Christianization of our community. We want to revive the *Koinonia* of the early church, as recorded in the Acts. This wonderful early Christian fellowship, based on a spontaneous practice of the principle of the Cross in social economics was too evanescent. Yet because of it the apostles were able to give their testimony to the Resurrection 'with great power.' We shall not regain the fullness of their Pentecostal experience until we have re-incarnated Incarnate Love in an organization of society embodying the best light that has been vouchsafed by the Spirit of God through the two thousand years of human labor and intellectual strivings." *The Missionary Review of the World,* Nov. 1931. p. 837.

[22]*Faith and Order,* Doran, 1927. Ed. by N. H. Bate. pp. 111-12.

[23]At times Luther could speak in similar words. "We also call the Roman Church holy in our day, and all its episcopal offices are holy, however misguided and however wicked the occupants thereof. Even though Rome is worse than Sodom and Gomorrah, there are nevertheless baptism, the sacrament, the Word of the gospel, the holy Scriptures, the offices of the church, the name of Christ and the name of the Church. The treasure is there for those who accept it; and they who do not accept it are without excuse, for it is at hand. Therefore the Roman Church is holy, since it has God's holy name, the gospel, baptism, etc. If a people has these it is called holy. So too our Wittenberg is a holy city, and we are in truth holy, since we are baptized, have received the eucharist, been instructed, and called by God. We have God's work in our midst, the Word and the sacrament. Through them we are holy." Quoted from *Commentary on Galatians* (I:2 WA. 40, 1, p. 69ff) by Gustav Aulen, "Lutheranism and the Unity of the Church" in *This Is the Church.* pp. 332-3. Ed. by A. Nygren. Philadelphia, Muhlenberg Press, 1952.

[24]*Origins of Christianity.* p. 185. See II:5.

[25]An example of a contemporary concern for the wholeness of a nation is Oliver Tomkins' *The Wholeness of the Church.* S C M Press, London, 1949.

[26]Bishop S. Neill has studied the whole field of church history from the viewpoint of the bearing of the church on social life in his recent *Christian Society* (Harper, 1953).

[27]cf. author's essay, "The Ministry and the Means of Grace." p. 21ff in *World Lutheranism of Today.* A Tribute to Anders Nygren. Stockholm, 1950.

[28]*The Second World Conference on Faith and Order.* Ed. by Leonard Hodgson, 1938. p. 225. See I:15.

[29]"The Catholicity of Lutheranism," Gustav Aulen, pp. 19-20 in *World Lutheranism of Today,* a Tribute to Anders Nygren, 1950.

III

The Catholic Church

ABOUT NO one of the four designations of the Church is there so much vagueness and uncertainty as that of the term "Catholic." Indeed, some communions which clearly declare their adherence to the Nicene Creed do not hesitate to change the word and substitute the word "Christian"—which, of course, makes no sense, for there can be no question of any other church in this Third Article of the Creed than the Christian Church. The change is defended on the ground that the word "Catholic" is in the popular mind identified with the Roman Church. But this defense reveals the curious history of the word. Meanwhile an important truth of the Christian faith is obscured, and Christians are left without a word to confess an essential fact about the Church. The ecumenical movement would do well to re-examine the concept of catholicity, and help all the churches to a clearer understanding of their attitude toward this quality of the Church of Christ.

The use of the word "Christian" as a translation of "Catholic" antedates Luther in German usage, but his selection of it gave it wide currency.[1] Not all Lutherans, however, followed him. The Swedish Church, for instance, has a word "allmännelig" which is rather a translation of the term "universal." Cranmer in 1549 used "Catholic" in the translation of the Creed, but in the Canon chose "universal." But neither "Christian" nor "universal" is a true rendering of the Greek καθολική, which referred to a quality of the Church, not to it geographical extent. There is little hope that either word can become acceptable for all the Church. What is to be desired is the renovation of the term "Catholic" and giving to it its original meaning.

It is a part of the apostolic character of the Church that its catholicity be interpreted in the light of both Old and New Testaments. For the "little flock" (Luke 12:32) of disciples of Jesus were from the first conscious of their relationship to the kingdom they were promised. They were no obscure band of religious enthusiasts, but the inheritors of an ancient hope and an eternal commonwealth. All the promises of God to the people of Israel belonged to them. They were included in God's plan for the redemption of the whole of mankind. It was no merit of their own that gave them this high estate. It was the grace of God which had made them worthy to be used of God for purposes which embraced all peoples and all times. They were early addressed as "an elect race, a royal priesthood, a holy nation, a people for God's own possession, that ye may show forth the excellencies of him who called you out of darkness into his marvellous light: who in times past were no people, but now are the people of God: who had not obtained mercy, but now have obtained mercy" (1 Peter 2:9).

The Christians of the New Testament, evidence amply reveals, considered the Church as the people of God who had entered into the inheritance of the Old Testament people of Israel. At the crucial conference in Jerusalem recorded in Acts 15, James refers to the point of transition when the Gentiles enter into a holy mission hitherto thought of as uniquely Israel's province. "Brethren," James asked, 'hearken unto me: Symeon hath rehearsed how first God visited the Gentiles, to take out

of them a people for his name. And to this agree the words of
the prophets; as it is written,

> After these things I will return,
> And I will build again the tabernacle of David,
>   which is fallen;
> And I will build again the ruins thereof,
> And I will set it up:
> That the residue of men may seek after the Lord,
> And all the Gentiles, upon whom my name is called,
> Saith the Lord, who maketh these things known from
>   of old"

(Acts 15:16.)

We know the early problem which the Church faced in bringing the Gentiles into the household of God. But rarely do we
notice how the Pauline conception of the Church implies a
reconciliation of Jew and Gentile which has not yet come to
pass. In the degree that the early Church became a Gentile
Church it lost something of its character of catholicity, for it
was meant to be a Church in which the faith of Jew and Gentile might become one. If we read Ephesians 2:11-22 in the
light of the purpose of God to create of Jew and Gentile "one
new man" we will catch a glimpse of Paul's conception of a
Catholic Church which from the first was eclipsed because of
the unbelief of the Jew. "The household of God" was the
apostle's description of the new people of Israel among whom
God would dwell, "a holy temple—for a habitation of God in
the Spirit." The history of redemption was the story of the re-
jection of Christ by his own people and of the acceptance of
him by the Gentiles in the hope that Israel would be saved
in the time of the "fullness of the Gentiles" (Rom. 11:25-26)—

a panorama that led the apostle to a cry of rhapsody, "O the depth of the riches both of the wisdom and the knowledge of God! How unsearchable are his judgments, and his ways past tracing out!" By its un-Christian treatment of the Jew in all centuries the Church has forfeited a significant part of a catholicity given it in the New Testament.

The catholicity of the New Testament consists in a view of the universality of the redemption in Christ. The Old Testament is caught up in it—the ages to come are a manifestation of its effect. The Epistle to the Hebrews pictures a sacrifice more universal than that of the old covenant and calls the roll of "a great cloud of witnesses" (ch. 11) who surround the Christians now come "to the general assembly and church of the first born who are enrolled in heaven" (12:23). John lifted his eyes from the discouragements of the seven churches to the great host in heaven, and heard the hymn of the elders before the Lamb,

> "Worthy art thou to take the book, and to open the seals thereof: for thou was slain, and didst purchase unto God with thy blood men of every tribe, and tongue, and people, and nation, and madest them to be unto our God a kingdom and priests" (Rev. 5:9).

At best there is no adequate explanation of the faith of the followers of Jesus who before his death believed themselves heirs of the kingdom of God and after his resurrection dared proclaim that all things centered in Christ. It is the miracle of the Church which no rationalism ancient or modern has been able to account for. But the New Testament is the indubitable witness of that faith—a faith that veritably conquered the world. The people whom Christ made to be this new Israel thought of

themselves as apostolic and holy, not because of their own quali-
fications, but because they were one with Christ, in whom are
all the treasures of wisdom and knowledge hidden" (Col. 2:3).
And since *all* fullness dwelt in him it was the will of God
"through him to reconcile *all* things unto himself—things upon
the earth, or things in the heavens" (1:19-20), and the duty of
the Church became one of "admonishing *every* man and teaching *every* man in *all* wisdom, that we may present *every* man
perfect in Christ" (v. 28). His Church was catholic because
Christ was given "all authority in heaven and on earth" and all
nations were to be His disciples (Matt. 28:18-19).

There can be little doubt that the New Testament speaks not
only of the particular local groups each of which formed a congregation, or ecclesia, but also of a Church in which all of
these were comprised. They were single, individual, units eligible
to call themselves a church because each exhibited those properties which belonged to the idea of the Church itself. Passages
occur in which something of the pre-existent Church is thought
of, which now manifests itself in the concrete congregations of
the time (Gal. 4:26, Phil. 3:20). But the relationship of the
local group is not only vertical—to the Head of the Church
and the heavenly community, but also horizontal—to each other,
wherever Christians might be found. "For it hath been the good
pleasure of Macedonia," Paul tells the Romans, "and Achaia to
make certain contributions for the poor among the saints that
are in Jerusalem" (Rom. 15:26). The churches of Galatia and
the Church of Corinth are instructed by Paul concerning "collec-
tion for the saints" (1 Cor. 16:1)—on a matter of this kind
Paul and his colleagues received appointment by the churches
(2 Cor. 8:19). Epistles circulated, as did teachers, among the

churches (Col. 4:16). Common to all the churches was the gospel which had been given them by the apostles—in this tradition they were exhorted to remain steadfast (2 Thess. 2:15). That which made them a Church was that which was theirs with all the saints, singly or in congregations, "one body, and one Spirit—one hope—one Lord, one faith, one baptism, one God and Father of all, who is over all, and through all, and in all" (Eph. 4:4-7).

Such is the New Testament chapter of the story of the word catholic. The centuries that followed witnessed a strange development of the idea. For whereas the New Testament Church thought of the gospel of Christ as catholic, bearing on all life, on all peoples, on all times, the idea soon came to be associated with a *form of government* within and above the congregations. We have seen that the New Testament cannot be made to prove the existence of any one church order. There were bishops and presbyters and deacons, but their relationship is nowhere defined, and it is most probable that areas differed in respect to the names and functions ascribed to presbyters and bishops. As far as the apostolic scriptures are concerned the important thing was a unity of message, and government is hardly mentioned. Certainly the form of government was not a part of the apostolic tradition, beyond the point that the apostles were concerned that a responsible leader be found in each congregation, who could answer for the contents of the message and the conduct of worship in which was included the administering of the sacraments.

The word "catholic" has a history in the second and third centuries which illustrates how the shift was made from a New Testament catholicity to one associated with an hierarchical organization centering in Rome. It first appears in the letters of Ignatius, the third bishop of Antioch, who suffered martyrdom in Rome early in the second century, probably in the reign of Trajan. He wrote to congregations which entertained him on his journey to Rome, and in his letter to the church in Smyrna these words occur, "See that you all follow the bishop, as Jesus Christ follows the Father, and the presbytery as if it were the Apostles. And reverence the deacons as the command of God. Let no one do any of the things appertaining to the Church without the bishop. Let that be considered a valid Eucharist which is celebrated by the bishop, or by any one whom he appoints. Wherever the bishop appears let the congregation be present; just as wherever Jesus Christ is, there is the Catholic Church. It is not lawful either to baptize or to hold an 'agape' without the bishop; but whatever he approve, this is also pleasing to God, that everything which you do may be secure and valid."[2] And the Trallians Ignatius admonished, "Let all respect the deacons as Jesus Christ, even as the bishop is also a type of the Father, and the p r e s b y t e r s as the council of God and the college of the Apostles (συνέδριον θεοῦ και ὡς σύνδεσμον ἀποστόλων). Without these the name of 'Church' is not given."[3]

These are classic statements and deserve close study, both for what is said and not said. We are apt to read into these words of the sub-apostolic period ideas of one or two centuries later. The language is to some extent figurative. To liken the relationship of congregation to bishop with that of Christ to the Father is to speak in figure, even if we grant that Ignatius was writing generations before the Christological discussions. Remarkably, in both passages the bishop is not correlated with the apostles—which is the later interpretation, but the presbytery is compared to the body of the apostles. The presbytery is "the sanhedrin (the Greek word) of God," and the "college of the apostles." While this passage enjoins the church from doing anything apart from the bishop, another passage in the letter to the Trallians claims that "whoever does anything apart from the bishop and the presbytery and the deacons is not pure in his conscience"[4]—here all three are joined together. Ignatius does not say that where the bishop is there is the Catholic Church, but "wherever Jesus Christ is, there is the Catholic Church," and this in parallelism to the phrase, where the bishop is there is the congregation, or the whole. We would be justified in interpreting the meaning to be that where Christ is there the fullness or wholeness of the Church is, and to see herein an allusion to the congregation at worship, that is, celebrating the Eucharist. In fact there is back of the language of Ignatius a view of the church gathered around its Lord as in the days of the apostles. The church at worship is in unity with its Lord, and the bishop stands there among the presbytery before the congregation as Christ stood with his apostles in the days he ministered to the multitudes. There is nothing of jurisdiction here and no question of hierarchy. A responsible leader of the eucharistic gathering of a congregation bears the name of bishop, and is the symbol of its unity. But how loosely Ignatius differentiates in his speaking of "types" is evident when in one moment he commands obedience to the bishop as the type of the Father, and in another says, "Let all respect the deacons as Jesus Christ." All that we can conclude from the famous letters of Ignatius is that in the sub-apostolic age presbytery and deacons joined with the bishop in ordering the worship and discipline and doctrine of the congregation.

We are confronted in Ignatius with the relationship of congregations to each other and the idea each congregation had of itself. The churches to which Ignatius wrote were mostly small communities ruled by presbytery and bishop and deacons. Their unity lay in themselves and was maintained by regular worship at which the bishop presided and by a community discipline and service administered by presbyters and deacons. Yet each was something more than a unit to itself. Each partook of a gospel which had relevance beyond itself, indeed to every community. Each was a representative of the people of God to whom were given the promises, the apostles, the sacraments. We can say that the Church was in each of them and each of them was in the Church. The Church as a people of God existed before any of these congregations—each became a Church as it participated in the possessions of the people of God. We are not now so much concerned with the relationship of each to the other—this soon became a problem—but with the relationship of each to Him who constituted the Church. Christians became members of the Church by their relation to the Head of the Church before their relation to other members. "Where Christ is, there is the Catholic Church," Ignatius asserts. He means only that the fullness of the Church, its integrity and its entirety, are in each congregation that has the possessions which reveal His presence. The officers of the congregation are responsible for the valid administration of the sacraments and the ministry of love which mark the church—they are types of the Trinity who dwell in the temple of believers. This is a "catholic" church—it possesses the whole gift of God in Jesus Christ.

As Zahn[5] contends, Ignatius speaks only of congregations at peace within themselves and blessed with good bishops. Heresy has not yet begun to divide these churches, at least they have been able to retain their unity, and the problem of unworthy bishops had not yet appeared. It was natural for the Syrian bishop to make every bishop a symbol of a congregation and to enjoin a congregation to be in harmony with its leader. More than this there is not in his letter. Certainly he makes no argument for the apostolic origin of bishops—he speaks rather of the presbyters as the successors of the apostles. He makes no distinction between the orders as to importance. He does not say that the Catholic Church is where the bishop is—the church is where Christ is. He does make clear that the local church is the manifestation of the entire Church.

As the congregations multiplied and came into relationships with each other they soon became conscious of the extent of the Church. They could begin to speak of the church as universal, in every place. This is the root meaning of the word "ecumenical." Just as we are apt to speak of some movement as soon as it reaches out as "international," or even "world-wide," so the Church could regard itself as universal in extent. But it is important to differentiate between universality or ecumenicity on the one hand and catholicity on the other. We might say that the first is horizontal in its measurement, the second vertical—one includes the world, the other reaches into the "heavenlies." But even this is inadequate, as we shall see, for catholic includes both the reference to the fullness of God in Christ, and the love of the household of faith which love to God implies. But emphasis is needed on the *qualitative* nature of catholicity as distinct from the quantitative element in universality.

Harnack sees in the middle of the second century the beginning of the substitution of the idea of universal for the more religious idea of the wholeness of the Church. Kattenbusch,[6] however, thinks that the fact that the Church did not use the term "ecumenical" or world-wide, indicates that it held on to the word "catholic" but gave it in practice another meaning. What really happened was that one type of organization prevailed over others, and became what we would call "standard." Until the third century there were relatively few bishops in Egypt.[7] In Asia Minor very large areas were under one bishop. In Gaul and Spain more than one city shared a bishop. The principle seemed to be that congregations should be related to some bishop rather than each have its own. By the middle of the third century, however, there was a rapid increase in number. At that time a synod in Rome brought together 60 bishops from Italy, and by the end of the century the Egyptian area had over 100 bishops. The episcopal organization had become the norm.

But for centuries the diocese was as autonomous as the early congregations had been. The necessity of combating heresy and the solidarity engendered by persecution were centripetal forces. Bishops were appointed by mother churches, which often were located in strategic political centers, and new dioceses felt themselves bound to their "mother" church. But there was no general pattern of inter-diocesan relationships until the time of the synods, and to this day the Greek churches of the various Eastern countries are independent of each other, except as they recognize a common Patriarch. In the West a combination of circumstances led to the priority of the See at Rome. But this was not more than a courtesy for the first two centuries, and is not defined even by the time of Cyprian, around 250 A.D. Irenaeus does in an ambiguous passage speak of respect due the see of Peter and Paul "propter potiorem principalitatem,"[8] but it is not in the sense that the other churches are subordinate to the Church in the capital, for these owed nothing to Rome, being indeed, many of them, older and more significant than that church in the formative years of the Church. Even Cyprian's celebrated "De Unitate" does not portray a hierarchichal organization ordered by Rome, and the bishop of Carthage disagreed with the Roman Church on the question of the re-baptism of lapsi. Cyprian did see the episcopal system as a bond of union, making possible inner communication and mutual agreement between scattered parts of the Church.

It is not necessary here to go beyond Nicea. Once the Church had entered into an alliance with the Imperial State, the episcopacy assumes an entirely different character. It now becomes an office, with legal standing and political power. By the end of the fourth century Ambrose[9] had transformed the power of a bishop and paved the way for the medieval development of the papacy—and a future Reformation. To say that this does not concern us is not to deny the importance of this development. But the farther we go, the farther we get away from the apostolicity of the Church. Even the Catholic nature of the Church must be determined by its apostolic character. Certainly there is little ground in Scriptures for the trend church organization took after Nicea, and we must confine our study of catholicity to the centuries when the Church was still free of governmental entanglement. The ante-Nicene Church presents us with a growing number of widely-spread churches seeking to proclaim the apostolic message and to find ways of relating themselves to each other. In a period of autocratic government such as the Roman Empire exhibited in the second and third centuries, it was natural that church government should be conceived in terms of provinces with centralized power, and that these provinces should look torward a central capital. The development from Ignatius to Cyprian is entirely in accord with the necessities of the age. But it is one thing to understand how the churches gradually formed themselves into larger units with loyalties to one or another center. It is quite another thing to make this a perpetual standard for the form of the Church, and to want to "go back" to some such historical situation.

It is my conviction that the wholeness of the Church, which the term "catholic" was originally meant to express, is an aspect of both the apostolicity and the holiness of the Church, and is not primarily concerned with a form of government. It has to do with government only insofar as the structure of the Church can be a means to the proclamation of the full, the whole, gospel. "Wherever Jesus Christ is, there is the Catholic Church." Christ was present with his people in the Eucharist wherever they gathered to be built up in faith. Paul's words to the elders of Ephesus portrays the apostolic succession of a ministry he had exercised but was now passing on: "And now I commend you to God, and to the word of his grace, which is able to build you up, and to give you the inheritance among all of them that are sanctified" (Acts 20:32). Here is an immediacy of the Word of grace, active in a congregation represented by its elders, which is dependent on neither local bishop or diocesan inter-relationships. The wholeness of the Church is inherent in the wholeness of Christ. The Church becomes catholic in the degree it grows into the fullness of Christ. Apostles, prophets, evangelists, pastors, teachers (bishops are not mentioned) in the Ephesian passage are secondary to "the perfecting of the saints." And the "work of ministering" is equated with "the building up of the

body of Christ" which has as its goal "the unity of the faith
and of the knowledge of the Son of God"—herein is the "full-
grown man," "the measure of the stature of the fulness of
Christ" (Eph. 4:11-13). To identify the catholicity of the
Church with a form of government of the third century is to
make of a means an end, and to raise to an absolute place
what is a relative form.

It has of course been argued that the episcopal system was a
guarantee of the apostolic message and discipline. As a matter
of fact the temptation was to regard it as a goal in itself, not
merely a means, and actually it guaranteed only the preserva-
tion of the episcopal system. For insofar as the bishop maintained the purity of doctrine he went back to the apostolic
standard of the Scriptures. He was not above that standard. It
judged him more than he judged it. And in matters of dispute
as to the application of the doctrine he felt it necessary to refer
these to synods. If the argument of the guarantee of true doctrine were valid, the very existence of the system should have
precluded all schism. The story of the relations of the Greek
and Roman churches in the earlier period and of the movements toward reform in the later Middle Ages is itself the story
of the inadequacy of the episcopal system to keep the Church
apostolic, holy, and catholic. The Reformation was the only re-
course open for the changing of a system that had absolutized
itself and set itself above the sovereignty of the apostolic ministry. The restoration of the whole gospel of Christ, the veritable
catholicity of the Church, was the aim of the Reformation. The
explosion wrecked a certain structure of organization which had
been reared in the house of God, and it removed partitions
which had been built between clergy and laity. But it gave free-

dom for the fullness of the gospel and opportunity for a unity of the congregation with Christ which was of the essence of the New Testament Church. It restored the Word as the supreme arbiter in the congregation. It may be claimed that the Reformation fell short of its aim. A contemporary Lutheran scholar admits that the Augsburg Confession nowhere pictures the Church in as wide a context as the New Testament places it. Asmussen emphasizes that the Church must be seen not per se, but as a phenomenon of the history of the world, of which it is a part, in fact, the central meaning. The Epistle to the Ephesians and the Book of Revelation reveal that "the mystery of the history of the Church is the real motive power of world history," and of this there is not a trace in the *Augustana*.[10] This is only to say that we have not yet thought through all the implications of the Reformation. We may, however, still hold that in the Reformation the Word was restored to its supreme place as arbiter over against any organization or office of the Church which made itself the measure of the Church. Even on this particular point it was not the episcopate which made possible a new evaluation of the relationship of church history to world history. Above the sufficiency of a worldly hierarchy rose the judgment of Ephesians and the Book of Revelation. The Spirit of God transcended in the Reformation Period as before it had in the New Testament an organized ministry which believed it guaranteed the truth of God.

How one-sided and misleading is the tendency to identify the catholicity of the Church with an episcopal organization may be seen when we examine the contributions of three other offices mentioned by the apostle and very prominent in the actual life of the Church.

First, the evangelist. And in the field of missions he is pre-eminent. We are apt to lose sight of him in church history, because the term becomes obscured, and attention is focused on the bishop's office. But it is the monk as evangelist who is the great builder of the church in the Middle Ages. The catholic quality of the church rightly suggests the expansion of the Church to all parts of the earth. Boniface, Ansgar, Willibrord, Augustine—the whole long line of missionary successors to the apostles testifies to the work of exploration and establishment by which the Church is spread throughout the world before a bishop appears on the newly won scene. In the Roman Church it was the Franciscans and Dominicans and, after the Reformation, the Jesuits and the Capuchins who brought the message of the Church to India and to California. The Protestant Church, as Latourette explains,[11] was slower in getting started but more than rivalled the Roman Church with its missionary advances after 1800, and was especially successful in establishing missions which in turn became sending-stations. Unique in Protestant missions is the part played by congregations and missionary societies, many or most of which had no episcopal connection and depended on the laity as much as on the clergy.[12] The succession of the apostolic messengers in the period of missionaries is as glorious a chapter as can be found in the history of the Church.

A very recent illustration of the centrality of the Word in the mission and life of the Church comes to us out of the East. In 1950 an important conference was held in Bangkok, at which the World Council and the International Missionary Council assessed the situation of the Christian Church in the East. There Marxism is threatening the very existence of those newly won provinces of the Church and from one of the great countries, China, Western missionaries have been driven out. On his return from the Bangkok Conference, Charles Ranson, general secretary of the International Missionary Council, had sobering things to say of the prospect of the Church in this 20th century persecution. "The answer to Marxism," he said, "the ultimate Christian answer, is a theological one. The answer is not in social theory—not even in the declaration of moral absolutes. It is a proclamtion of the truth that the world has a Lord, a Judge, and a Savior, Jesus Christ, and that only in the acknowledgment of that Lord, who stands outside and judges history, can human rights ultimately be safeguarded and human justice ultimately be achieved." And the kind of apostolic succession that counts in this hostile environment is a succession of witnesses, this informed observer asserts, as he declares that "one of the things that struck me almost everywhere I went among the churches in Asia is that many of those churches are heavily professionalized. There is a dangerous and heretical form of clericalism which regards the task of preaching the Gospel and spreading the Word as the prerogative of the paid and full-time ministry of the Church. A professionalized Church will not stand in the day of trial. The only kind of church that will be able to resist the pressures of social sentiment or political action is a church in which every member is a witness to his faith in Christ. We need a revival of lay activity that will carry the message of the Gospel out onto the frontiers where men do their jobs, in contact with the realities of modern society and of the contemporary world. It is not without significance that the great community movements in India have for the most part been movements of lay witness."[13]

Second, the teacher. Catholicity may be thought of too exclusively in geographical terms. The wholeness of the Church includes the adequacy of its gospel for all of human life. Throughout its long career the Church has had to wage combat continually against those who would restrict the gospel to so small a part of human experience that large areas are untouched.[14] Learning, art, business, recreation—each has at some time or in some religious groups been branded as worldly and outside the realm of redemption. Some peoples have considered themselves peculiar objects of God's grace and others as "heathen." Some callings have been glorified as "holy," while others are "secular." The comprehensiveness of the gospel has never been as zealously represented as its applicability to individuals. In no section of the church has catholicity of sympathy been as consciously emphasized as the advantages of particularism. But it is the Christian teacher in every communion who has lifted the eyes of the individual to the bearing of faith on politics, on science, on history, on the arts. The *bishop* of Hippo is of less consequence than the *author* of the *City of God* in giving the gospel dimensions as wide as those of human history. Thomas of Aquinas has left a deathless heritage in his view of all truth centering in the revelation of Jesus Christ. It was as *teachers* of the Church that the greatest leaders of Protestantism preserved a succession of truth to the ages—Luther, Calvin, Knox (not one of whom was a bishop.) Newton and Linnaeus comprehended a system of laws of Nature within a creation of the Christian God which refutes the modern gnostics who cannot believe that the creator of the universe is the Father of our Lord Jesus Christ. And we are still fumbling in the dark in our attempt to find a way to reconcile the laws of social life with the laws of God though there is no area of human life where that law does not apply. The Word of God is not only that in Jesus Christ "we have our redemption through his blood" and "the forgiveness of our trespasses" but a revelation of the purpose of God "to sum up all things in Christ, the things in the heaven and the things upon the earth" (Eph. 1:3-10).

Third, the deacon. This humble office has in all ages been associated with the ministry of mercy. There is a succession in this ministry which stretches from the early Church, through care of sick and aged, orphan and widow, homeless and deserted, down to our own days of ministry to the displaced and the war refugee. Love never faileth—it leaps across confessional boundaries and witnesses more effectively to the wideness of God's mercy than many other messengers of His grace. Women —be they in the tradition of St. Clara or of Florence Nightingale or the deaconesses of Kaiserswerth and Bielefeld—have exemplified in a peculiar way the catholicity of the Church. The Salvation Army might well claim the deacon's title in modern church history. Neither faith nor love can be channeled in any organization of the Church so as to restrict it to a human scheme. The Church is the well from which gushes the waters of mercy, but the diaconate cannot be held within the bounds of a system. Paul in Romans 13:4 calls even the state "a deacon of God," ministering to the welfare of the citizen, and Polycarp, in his letter to the Philippians places before deacons the example of Christ, the "deacon of all" (v. 2).

Yet when all this has been said as to offices in the Church we must also recognize the place of the episcopate through the centuries. After the second century this form of organization prevailed and became universal in the Eastern Church until our day, and in the Western countries until the Reformation. Due weight must be allowed the fact that even today the majority of Christians are under bishops, in the Orthodox, the Roman, the Old Catholic Churches and in the Church of England, the Church of Sweden, and in certain other Protestant countries. Nor can even the most ardent non-episcopal communion hope that these churches will divest themselves of this order for the sake of a united Church without bishops. We need to understand what the episcopate is as well as what it is not. It is an historic order which is inextricably interwoven with the life of the Church. So dominant has this system been that even those who oppose it must describe the functions of the presbytery or the congregation in terms of a substitute for episcopal functions. The ecumenical spirit cannot therefore depreciate what the bishopric has been and still is in the churches of Christ.

The area of disagreement can be reduced to this point—is the historic episcopate essential for a Church wherein Christians have fellowship with one another? Since it is almost everywhere granted that unity in the Church requires apostolic sanction, this question resolves itself into this—is the episcopate based on undoubted scriptural authority? If not it will have to rest on a foundation of tradition, in which case it cannot be considered a requirement for every part of the Church. This is the position I believe is warranted both by New Testament exegesis and the history of the Church. In other words it is not necessary that all churches adopt the episcopate in order to achieve unity. It is conceivable that episcopal and non-episcopal communions could have fellowship with each other, each recognizing the ministry of the other and expressing their fellowship in inter-communion despite the differences of ministry.

This is not to overlook the difficult question of validity of sacraments, the episcopal advocate questioning the administration of sacraments by a ministry not ordained by a bishop in historic succession. But such administration of baptism is generally admitted, and the Orthodox theory of "Economy" even recognizes the ordination[15] of ministers coming from other communions. A unity among churches with different ministries would mean that an apostolic administration of sacraments required agreement as to the scriptural nature of the sacrament rather than as to the ministry administering it. In a sense this would be no more than an extension of the anti-donatist doctrine—the validity of the sacrament is no more effected by the manner of the minister's ordination than by his character.

In any event it is hard to see any prospect of advance in ecumenical unity until the question of the episcopate is removed from the realm of the apostolic essence of the Church and made a matter of tradition and of choice, respected where maintained but not deemed necessary for the existence either of a church or church fellowship.[16]

Is it not apparent that our own views of the Church, and of the ministry of the Church, are far less universal and all-embracing than those the New Testament unfolds? A catholic church is a church where apostles, prophets, evangelists, teachers, all minister to the saints "unto the building up of the body of Christ—in love," but we dare apply the adjective only to a Church which has "the fullness of Christ." The fullness of Christ includes "not only this world—but that which is to come" (Eph. 1:21). It includes the church in heaven as well as on earth.

The Greek church correctly interprets the Eucharist as a communion not only of living members of the congregation with
their Head but also with the departed saints. The whole church
of Christ cannot be seen at one time or place. Nor can the fullness of the Church be apparent in this aeon of time. The confession of catholicity is thus a confession in the eschatological
Church—the Church of eternity. It is a confession that the
Church transcends place and time and encompasses all places
and all times. There is no more breath-taking description of the
Church than this, and in it is implicit man's faith in the unity
of mankind, and of time and eternity.[17]

The Greek Church may well aid us in a clearer understanding of catholicity by its reference to a quality it calls "Sobornost"
and which it defines in the original biblical sense of the word
catholic. Professor Florovsky has emphasized that "the conception of catholicity cannot be measured by its world-wide expansion; universality does not express it exactly. Καθολική means,
first of all, the inner wholeness and integrity of the Church's
life." "The Church," he holds, "is a unity not only in the sense
that it is one and unique; it is a unity, first of all, because its
very being consists in reuniting separated and divided mankind.
It is this unity which is the 'sobornost' or catholicity of the
Church. This is the mystery of the final reunion in the image
of the Unity of the Holy Trinity." And of the unity of individuals he says, "the gauge of catholic union is that 'the multi-
tude of them that believe be of one heart and of one soul.'
Where this is not the case, the life of the Church is limited
and restricted. The ontological blending of persons is, and must
be, accomplished in oneness with the Body of Christ; they cease
to be exclusive and impenetrable."[18]

Can we hope to restore to the creed of the Church a declaration of this kind of faith in the Church of Jesus Christ? I can interpret the lack of this profession only as a weakness of the Church. Not to use the word because it is misleading is to confess that we lack more than the right word—we lack the thing the word represents. To the degree that this characteristic is obscured the Church is itself in eclipse. Nor can there be a true unity of the Church when one vital dimension of it is neither clear nor professed. There have been revivals in the Church to restore its apostolicity and to stress its holiness. May I suggest that the ecumenical movement is, by the grace of God, a revival in Christendom to regain for our profession of Christian faith the element of fullness which no fraction of the Church by itself can exemplify? To believe in the wholeness of the Church one must believe in the ecumenical endeavor, for it testifies to a Christ who is above us all. Though it did not use the word the Affirmation of Edinburgh in 1937 was couched in catholic terms when it declared, "We are *one* because we are *all* the objects of the love and grace of God, and called by Him to witness in *all* the world to His glorious gospel."[19]

NOTES

[1]WA 30:I, p. 130 Note 3, quotes a gloss of Luther, 1538, in *Die drei Symbola*, "Christlich. 'Catholica' kann man nicht wohl besser deutschen denn "cristlich,' wie bisher geschehen, das ist wo Christen sind in aller welt." Reference is made to the use of the term "Christlich" for "Catholica" in Surgant's *Manual*, and in *Vocabularius predicantium* von 1482.

[2]*Apostolic Fathers*, trans by K. Lake, Macmillan (Loeb Library) 1914, vol. I:261.

[3]Ibid. I:215.

[4]Ibid. I:219.

[5]Theodore Zahn, *Ignatius von Antiochien* (Gotha, 1873). pp. 437ff.

[6]F. Kattenbusch. *Verbreitung und Bedeutung des Taufsymbols* (Leipzig, 1900). II:924-5.

[7]*Kirchengeschichte*, by Karl Müller, Tubingen, 1924. I:305-6.

[8]*Ante-Nicene Fathers*, vol. I. p. 415.

[9]Berkhov, Henrik, *Kirche und Kaiser*, Zurich, 1947, clearly shows that the political power of the episcopate dates from Ambrose.

[10]*Warum Noch Lutherische Kirche?* Hans Asmussen, Stuttgart, 1949. pp. 58, 117.

[11]Introductory chapter, in vol. III (Three Centuries of Advance, A.D. 1500-1800) of *History of the Expansion of Christianity*, Harper, 1939. "Protestants were bringing into being new instruments for propagating the Christian faith. The societies which they were forming were without exact precedent in the expansion of Christianity, or indeed, in the spread of any religious faith. They were organizations, not purely of the clergy, but in which clergy and laity joined." (p. 50.)

[12]Ernst Benz in *Die Ostkirche Und Die Russische Christenheit* (Tübingen, 1949), p. 63ff., has given a similar picture of the missionary method of the Church in Russia.

[13]"Towards a Christian Strategy in East Asia," a pamphlet, 1950. Charles W. Ranson.

[14]Over a century ago Franz von Baader traced the rise of Nihilism, both Western and Russian, to the modern divorce of knowledge and faith, and called for a restoration of their unity. Ernest Benz. "Nihilism—In West and East," in *The Lutheran Quarterly*, Feb. 1950. pp. 17-33.

[15]George Florovsky, "The Doctrine of the Church and the Ecumenical Problem" in *The Ecumenical Review*, II:2. pp. 152-161.

[16]cf. articles by Francis Gray and Henri D'Espine, in *The Ecumenical Review*, IV, 2, and by A. G. Hebert, Ibid, IV, 3.

[17]cf. Hj. Lindroth, "The Dogma Concerning the Church," in *This Is the Church*, Ed. by A. Nygren, trans. by C. C. Rasmussen, Phila. Muhlenberg Press, 1952. pp. 181-3. Of Irenaeus Lindroth says that "that universalism which the Old Testament prophets already joined with the thought of the people of God, God's *ecclesia*, was seen in its fulness by the first great theologian of the ancient church."

[18]G. V. Florovsky, "Sobornost: The Catholicity of the Church" in *The Church of God*, Ed. by E. L. Mascall (S. P. C. K., London, 1934). pp. 55ff.

[19]*Faith and Order*, Edinburgh, 1937. p. 275.

IV

The Unity of the Church

IT WOULD be a mistake in these days of ecumenical interest to suppose that the reunion of the churches was a modern phenomena, and that we in our century first caught a vision of one church. Contemporary writers like McNeill in his *Unitive Protestantism* and Charles Clayton Morrison in his Hoover lectures *The Unfinished Reformation* have reminded us that it is more correct to view the Reformation as an attempt to unify than to divide the Western Church. Every century, in fact, since the Reformation has its representatives championing a reunion of the churches.

In the sixteenth century Martin Bucer, the Strassburg Reformer, strove ceaselessly to bring together the forces led by Luther and Zwingli. He sought for formulae which could bridge the differences that Marburg had discovered to be impassable. If anything can be learned from his vain labors it is that phraseology will not heal differences which are more than verbal.[1]

Later in the century (1565) Jacob Acontius,[2] an Italian humanist who found his way to Elizabeth's England via Switzerland, Strassburg, and Holland, tried to persuade his contemporaries that "pietas superat doctrinam"—piety takes precedence over doctrine. The title of his book, *Stratagemata Satanae*, expresses his belief that it is Satan who has persuaded men to make doctrine supreme. Not that all doctrine is secondary. Acontius distinquishes between principal doctrines necessary to salvation, and doctrines not necessary. The latter, he feels, are too prominent in the thinking of sects. The former, which are necessary, are few and must be based directly on Scripture. Acontius settled in London, and his distinction between doctrines influenced Richard Baxter in his *Saints' Everlasting Rest.*

George Calixtus,[3] in the middle of the 17th century, proposed another basis for the union of the churches of the Reformation and Rome. The ecumenical creeds and the theology of the first five centuries seemed to him to be sufficient—their acceptance by the believer would constitute him a member of the Church, and the churches should agree on them. He travelled widely in Germany, Belgium, France, and England, and gained fame by his disputation with a Jesuit, but the churches were unwilling to adopt a program they termed syncretistic.

A disciple of Calixtus, Gerard Molanus, the Lutheran abbot of Loecum, was drawn into negotiations with Roman theologians in the last quarter of the 17th century. Political considerations were clearly involved but the *Cogitations* of Molanus indicate how far the school of Melanchthon was willing to go to effect reunion with Rome. Another council was to be called, superseding Trent. "To insure the Protestants a canonical place in the council the pope should consecrate all Protestant superintendents as bishops and these bishops should be summoned to the council and sit as judges with an unrestricted suffrage along with the Roman bishops."[4] In a later work Molanus himself retreated from this position.

Even more zealous and cosmopolitan was a contemporary of Calixtus, namely John Dury.[5] Born in Scotland, at school in Holland and France and England, this Scotch-Presbyterian minister in Prussia knew at first hand the divisions of the church in

Holland, the French Huguenots, and the Anglican church. He came into contact with Gustavus Adolphus and in response to a challenge of a Swedish official he gave the next half century of his life to the cause of church unity. In two tracts he stated his views and program. He did not think doctrinal views alone caused the religious discord of Germany. Beside varieties of ceremonies and practices, he blamed the intemperate zeal of pastors for dispute, and thought some should be deposed for the good of the Church. He would have Lutherans and Reformed compose their internal differences, and then have a General Assembly called, representing churches from various countries. This assembly would establish a common creed, common worship, and standards of life—in fact a new church to be presided over by one Lutheran and one Anglican.

Both Calixtus and Dury were moved by the distress caused by the Thirty Years' War to consider ways of reconciling the opposing churches. Most famous of those whom these war conditions turned toward reflection on church unity was the philosopher Leibniz.[6] Few have had more ambitious plans than those he proposed for the reunion of Evangelicals and Romans and Greeks. All, he judged, were guilty of a lack of love. The conflicting doctrines were capable of reconciliation. But a will for unity must be present. The Roman Church would have to remove its Tridentine anathemas of the Protestants—the Protestants should acknowledge the headship of the Pope. In his view a hierarchy and a head were essential for the unity of the Church. Good will and a broad sympathy characterized this philosophical approach to the problem, but neither in his own lifetime nor later have his proposals received very serious consideration.

All of these efforts, up to this point, were the concern of individuals. In the 19th century an advance is marked by the formation of associations which definitely seek or imply a common interest of Christians in unity. Zinzendorf and the Moravian Brethren of the former century had spread seeds far and wide, which bore fruit in many places and forms. The growth of missionary societies in the early 19th century provoked thought on the common Christian message to be brought to newer regions. Churches everywhere began to attack social porblems such as slavery, temperance, war, and societies organized in these causes brought Christians together across denominational lines. The Y.M.C.A. became a world organization. The middle of the century was a time of harvest for the many plantings of interchurch co-operation, and a new spirit of fellowship was abroad.

Most effective in its attempts to bring churchmen from various lands together to consider the unity of Christendom was the Evangelical Alliance, whose story has not yet been fully told.[7] The Congregationalists of England seem to be the first church group to take action. John Angell James, a Congregationalist pastor of Birmingham, published as early as 1842 a book on *Christian Fellowship,* and in May of that year he proposed a union of all evangelicals at a meeting of the annual Congregational Union in London. A public meeting in Exeter Hall, in 1843, was attended by 4,000 people and it is said that a crowd of twice that number could not gain admission. It was at this meeting that James uttered a statement often echoed in our time, namely, "We are not assembled to create or establish unity, but to acknowledge that unity which already exists."

But the Congregationalists were not alone in calling for a restudy of the relationships of churches to each other. Theodore

Kniewel, an archdeacon of Danzig in 1842 visited England, France, Belgium, and Switzerland to awaken interest in a union of all evangelicals. Robert Balmer, in 1843, on the occasion of the Free Church of Scotland's observance of the Westminster Assembly anniversary, pleaded for greater fellowship and inspired the publication of *Essays on Christian Union* in 1845. This volume contained a letter of W. Patton of New York, calling for an international conference of all evangelicals. 55 Scotch pastors and laymen arranged for a meeting in Liverpool, which was held in October 1845 and attracted 216 delegates from 19 denominations. They proposed a meeting of world evangelicals for the Fall of 1846 on a platform that none was to give up his own confession, and that this was to be a union of Christians, not of churches. Eight articles were agreed upon as a "minimum belief." In general the movement was directed against Romanism and rationalism.

The Evangelical Alliance was organized Aug. 19, 1846 in London, when 922 delegates or participants, from 50 denominations responded to the Liverpool call. The majority were Methodists and Presbyterians, some were low Anglican churchmen. There were 80 Baptists and a dozen Lutherans. Great Britain was the home of most, America sent the second largest delegation. Other countries represented were Holland, France, Switzerland, Germany, and Sweden. About one-third were laymen. From the first it was clear that this was not to be a new church, or an organization interfering with any church, but a fellowship across the boundaries of churches, or, as it was termed, it was to be "a public exhibition of Christian love." The General or World Alliance was constituted of district organizations, each of which in its own country was autonomous.

In reality the central or World Alliance had no power, and the national groups became separate and independent. There were seven of them—Great Britain, the United States, France-Belgium-French Switzerland, North Germany, South Germany-German Switzerland, British North America, West Indies.

It is not necessary here to follow the fortunes of the Alliance which held international gatherings in various countries. James, in one of the public sessions of the London meeting, expressed the motto in words reminiscent of a 17th century author: "In things essential unity, in things non-essential liberty, in all things charity."[8] The proposal of the Alliance for a week of universal prayer each New Year's week was probably the most widely accepted of its measures. Most of the support for the Alliance came from the free churches. There can be no doubt that it was an aid to lay work, and one gets the impression that the program of the Alliance—especially its Conferences, afforded a rare opportunity for the training of Christian laymen on a world scale.

We have dwelt on the movement at this length partly to remind ourselves of the extent of this success a century ago, so that we see in proper perspective the achievements of the ecumenical movement of our own day—for which the Alliance was a sort of prologue. But also it is of importance to notice the nature of the Alliance—a free gathering of Christian individuals. Churches as such were not involved—therein is the important difference from the efforts of our day leading to a World Council of Churches. But it is a question if the churches of our day would have been prepared for a World Council if the ground had not been broken and important lessons had not been learned in the World Alliance.

We may then divide the movement for church unity into these three periods, since the Reformation—the period of individuals, speculating on ways of bringing the churches together, the period of associations, actually exhibiting co-operation of Christian individuals, and the period of the World Council of Churches, involving the churches in inter-church fellowship. This latter is the period since 1910 and includes the story of Stockholm, Lausanne, Oxford, Edinburgh, Amsterdam, Lund, and Evanston. Of these events I shall not speak, for they are within our own experience. But I return to our theme, to consider the meaning of the unity of the Church, in the light of the whole history of the Church. Our faith in the holiness, the catholicity, and the apostolicity of the Church must itself judge the validity of the concrete proposals we make for the reunion of Christendom. These attempts in themselves are meaningless except as they take into account the nature of the Church.

For the history of the Christian Church bears witness to the fact that unity is itself not an absolute. Were we to judge the mass of material which has been produced on the topic of church unity we might charge that much of it is superficial because it treats only of unity. There is a tacit assumption that the great wound or evil or scandal of the Church lies in the fact that it is not *one,* and that the mere organizing of it into some form of monopoly would heal its wounds, cure its evil, remove the scandal. It is my conviction that this is a futile approach to the problem. The unity of the Church is a unity of holiness, a catholic and apostolic unity, and the foregoing has attempted to give the contents I believe belong to these concepts. In short the only unity worth considering is the unity not merely of the Church, as a structure, but of the character of the Church as holy, catholic, and apostolic. Is such unity possible? To that question we would address ourselves in concluding this series of studies.

One illusion needs to be removed from our thinking before we try to see the true nature of the Church's unity, namely, that in all the centuries of Christianity there has ever been a period of an undivided Church, in the sense of one all-embracing organization. This is a legend, and to speak of a return to a period of the undivided Church is to pursue a legend. Sometimes this romantic period is placed in the late Middle Ages, but on nearer approach we see immediately that the whole of the period had its divisions and schisms. Or is the Inquisition a phenomena of the unity of the Church? And is the unity of the Church dependent on the relationship of the Church to the secular power with which the papacy is ever in league? Sometimes the golden period is thought of as existing in the earlier centuries. But when did all the Greek churches admit the monarchic primacy of Rome? And is the unity of the Church to be purchased at the expense of all those sects whose only divergence was that they took more seriously than did the majority the rule of holiness among the disciples of Christ? The Church organization that did prevail can of course boast of its unity, but was it a unity among the like-minded rather than the unity of the people of God? There is, in fine, no golden period of an undivided Christendom to which we can either look back or return. Such romantic dreams are as dust in the eyes of those who try to see the nature of the unity of an apostolic, holy and catholic Ecclesia.

In reality there has never been a united Church in the sense of one all embracing organization in which each part has functioned in a right relationship to the whole or to the other parts.

It is a fact too rarely observed that the "unions" of church history have mainly been forced by secular governments. Even the ecumenical councils of the early centuries were under the aegis of the Emperor. The attempts at councils of reunion in the later ages were as much politically inspired as religiously. Nor is this a phenomenon only of the pre-Reformation era. Princes and city councils were deeply involved in the formulation of the confessional statements of Lutherans, Calvinists, Anglicans. A contemporary statement on "Catholicity" by a commission of the Church of England frankly admits that "The post-Reformation Church of England was not the result of a theology. Political expediency played a large part in the shaping of its course, and in the determining of certain of its characteristics."[9] Indeed, one may wonder whether there has ever been a time in the history of the Church when the fellowship of communions could be effected without political entanglements before our own time when the church has won sufficient freedom from the state to make its own decisions. We are not going back, in the ecumenical endeavor, to something once existent and now lost. Rather we are feeling for a kind of fellowship in which the love of Christ is the constraining power, and where each part voluntarily brings its contribution to a whole which comprehends all the life of Christendom.

This is not to say that the modern freedom of the Church has by itself made for a unity among churches. It is necessary to observe that the connection of church and state is a symbol of the unifying function of the gospel in human life. Spokesmen and defenders of the state-church connection, as in England and Sweden,[10] view this relationship as an index of the bearing of the gospel on political and economic life in the nation. They are no less anxious for the full interpretation of the Christian message than those in the free churches who have stressed the social implications of Christianity. They come to think of the Church as bound up with the life of a nation in a way that may, under certain conditions, justify ties with the state. In some cases the ecumenical movement has found its leaders in churches which stress the Church as an institution offering the gifts of grace to all people rather than the Church as a communion of the faithful. In such churches there may be more tolerance and freedom for differences of doctrine than in closely bound confessional groups.

But even in state churches today there is a recognition of the independence of the Church which seeks ever more expression without sundering the tie with the state. In America we are witnessing attempts of the church to influence the state without involvement in state control. Both movements have the same motive—to bring the unifying power of the Church to bear on national life. What is new in the ecumenical conversations of today is the recognition that the unity of the Church is not dependent upon political factors.[11]

The divisions of the Church with which we are mainly concerned are those which have expressed the faith of Christians in an apostolic message, or a holy life, or a catholic fellowship. The medieval Church is a fair example of what happens when these other qualities are sacrificed for a unity of organization. In one form or another, in varying degrees, the denominations have preserved some true possession of the Church which, without their protest, was in risk of being lost. Ordinarily the protestants have been severed, as in the Reformation, from the older communion. Yet that communion is not the same as before, often yielding to its critics by not going farther in the direction that caused the split. And who can imagine what the Church would be today if all attempts at change had been successfully suppressed by a structure which placed unity above all? Not only the Church of Rome, but the Church of England and the Church of Sweden have tried to maintain a unity of office and of worship but each has failed. Church history is to so great an extent a story of failure to contain the Church in one form that the ecumenical movement of our day is destined to fail if its aim is to set up some one human authority over all the people of God. The existence of denominations is the result of historic situations which cannot be cancelled out merely by considerations of ecclesiastical uniformity.[12] The form which these denominations took was determined by what they stood for. The substance of their movement is of paramount importance, and there is no guarantee that an imposition of a universal organization would remove the real reason for the existence of the communions now separated.

We must allow that communions have arisen because they have believed that they were more fully obedient to the apostolic faith than was the body which had nourished them. The Waldensians in Italy, the Presbyterians and Congregationalists in England, the Lutherans in Germany, the Swiss Brethren in Zurich, the Mennonites in Holland, the Brethren in Moravia, the Methodists and Baptists in Great Britain and Scandinavia—by what definition of the Church are these to be excluded any more than the Anglicans and Greek Orthodox from the Catholic Church?

Is there, then, no hope for greater fellowship between those who differently interpret the word of the Lord and the sacraments in which He unites Himself with His followers? Is my conclusion merely an apologia for a divided Christendom, and a passive acceptance of a status which cannot be accepted as Christ's will for His people?

By no means. It is an attempt to steer away from blind alleys in our pursuit of unity, and to learn from the experience of the past what may not be hoped for in the reunion of Christendom. I accept the denominations as they are. I take them to be what they profess to be. We shall advance from where we are, which means a full recognition of what each stands for as its faith. It may not be ours. But neither may we deny the name of Christian to any who believe in a holy, catholic, apostolic church.

Our hope for the future lies in each one adding a new dimension to the scope of his faith. Here is no demand for reducing our faith, or giving up anything we hold precious. But I claim each of us must add something to a faith which is defective in holiness, in apostolic truth, and the fullness of Christ. Our unity will increase in the measure that we grow in these qualities. This is the direction in which unity lies.

The unity of the Church is a unity in Christ. The great moments in Christian history are those in which the apostolic message has been extended or purified or more fully interpreted. Not only in the Gospel of John (ch. 17) but repeatedly since, the unity of the Church has been associated with the apostolic mission. The first missionary wave of the early church brought the message to the Mediterranean world and established a faith which overcame the idolatry of Greece and Rome. The revelation of the nature and purpose of God in Jesus Christ became a unifying force around which a new culture gradually formed.

Missionaries from East and West made the Western world a
Christian world at least to the extent that in the biblical message a new center of human thought had been created. Again
in later centuries the apostles of the faith carried the gospel to
Asia and the New World, first in the Roman and then the
Protestant wave. Whatever the differences among the missionaries there was a witness to the Christ of the Gospels which
challenged the idolatry of ancient peoples of civilized lands and
pagan areas. The unifying force of all these centuries of missions has been the gospel of the Bible. The profession of faith
in an apostolic church has not been altogether vain—there has
been a teaching of the nations based on a message which has
come to the Church through the biblical relevation. And when
today the representatives of the younger churches meet in ecumenical conferences with those of the older, this itself is a proof
of the unity and the unifying power of the apostolic message
of Jesus Christ. The Theological Commission of the Lund Conference (1952) spoke for the whole church when it said, "Every
communion holds that the Church is not a human contrivance,
but God's gift for the salvation of the world, that the saving
acts of God in Christ brought it into being, that it persists in
continuity in history by the presence and power of the Holy
Spirit."[13]

But what advance can be made in bringing these various
communions, who all claim apostolic sanction, together for more
effective witness to the oneness of life in the one Lord, Jesus
Christ? Spener in his *Pia Desideria* has a remarkable section in
which he discusses the prevalence of dogmatic disputations in his
age as one of the ills afflicting the Church. He admits the need
of each one to state his view of the truth, but claims that

human pride, desire to defeat an adversary, and self glory often are the motives of disputants rather than love of truth.[14] "It is clear," he wrote, "that disputing is insufficient either to preserve the truth among ourselves or to win over those in error. The love of God is our need. Oh that we evangelicals really were deeply concerned about bringing to God heart-felt love as the fruit of His truth, and by showing forth such a conduct in our calling as to reveal a conscious, genuine love toward our neighbor and those we believe in error."[15] Do we exaggerate when we say that no Christian communion has excelled in proclaiming this part of the apostolic truth, namely, "the greatest of these is love"? Churches have used every instrument of power at their command to crush what they have believed to be error except what the Scriptures call the greatest of all weapons, Christian love!

> Det intet finns
> Som inte vinns
> Av kärleken som lider

runs a Swedish psalm verse, which might be translated freely,

> Nothing is found
> That is not won
> By love that suffers.

There is a unity of love which cannot be left out in any consideration of the true faith. All too often that faith has been made into an intellectual formula which is to be defended at all costs, and Christian piety is measured by the vehemence with which that truth is supported. But the faith that bears the name of Jesus Christ is confessed not by word alone, but by the life of the confessor. Confessions which have to be established by the power of the earthly sword have little resemblance to the confessions of saints who by their life and deeds prove the existence of Christ.

The deeper unity of the churches calls for a fuller exhibition of the love of God, which may be only another way of stressing the need of the Church to be holy. Churches which love to quote the opening words of the 5th chapter of Paul's letter to the Romans "Being therefore justified by faith," should read on to the end of the sentence, "because the love of God hath been shed abroad in our hearts through the Holy Spirit which was given unto us."[16] Granting Calvin's dictum that unity of affection is conditioned on unity in faith, we must not interpret that faith to include every minute point of dogma. Christians have no scriptural right to deny the name of fellow Christian to those who bear witness to Christ as their Lord and Saviour. The love that we owe the household of faith cannot be confined within the walls of that room which we occupy in the household. When we restrict love to the boundaries of the intellectual definition of our faith, we have made Christianity a smaller thing than the Scriptures make it. This is the peril of denominationalism, that it would limit the love of God to its own dimensions.

The obligation of the Church is to witness to an "unspeakable—infinite" grace of God in Jesus Christ. This is the other dimension which we said each communion must seek to possess. We must witness to a Christ beyond ourselves, greater than our faith. Our aim must not be to win all others to our communion but by our preaching and example lead others to consider with ourselves a fellowship more commensurate with the gospel we obey. The denomination is not an end in itself, but a means to an end beyond the present condition. That denomination is greatest among us which best exemplifies the service of God to mankind in Christ. Led by the Spirit of God such denominations can approach the catholic nature of the Church, wherein the fullness of Christ becomes apparent to all.

The opposite of catholic is sectarian, divisive, fractional. The opposite of wholeness, health, is a defect in some part. It is not in the part itself that the defect lies, for in this life all is partial, but it is the character of the part which is important. It is conceivable that the entire body of Christians might be organized into one system and the Church yet be without the wholeness of love, understanding, forgiveness, which is essential for the quality of unity. Justification exists for the division of Christians into local units, even into national units, when historic circumstances have so ordered it, but there is no justification for the animosity which characterizes these units in their relationship to each other, and for the harsh and often false judgments they make against each other. One can be so concerned about defending the truth of one's position that the spirit of that defence puts one out of the Christian community itself. Love of truth may become a garment that covers love of oneself and all our affirmations of "Lord, Lord" may not save us from the judgment of Him who does not know us, if we will not recognize our brethren in the faith.

Let a church set as its goal to teach its members the limitless love of God and a Christian attitude toward every man who bears the name of Christ and we will have an example of a Church seeking to be a truly Catholic church. That spirit can be found in even a small part of the Church, or even in an individual, as Tennyson's sum of truth was reflected in the flower. In the hues of such reflections of an all-embracing love we might behold the rainbow of hope, which betokens a Church in which the nations of the world might find unity. Compared to the creation of a true ecumenical spirit *within* the churches the devising of an organization *between* the churches is simple, yet there is no complete Church of Christ when the love of the Church is but a detached and isolated segment of the love of Christ. No member of the body of Christ lives to itself alone. Whether we acknowledge it or not, incorporation into His Body places us in relationship to all others in the body, and no denial of fellowship on our part can rend the unity of the Body—it can only separate us from the fullness of grace dwelling in the integration of the members in unity. If we are planted in the vine, the branches are not detached from other branches except those that bear no fruit—and each leaf and twig and limb derives strength through each other from the vine itself.

An appeal to the words of Christ, "Where two or three are gathered together in my name, there am I in the midst of them" (Matt. 18:20) is almost universal in the stories of separating churches. But the abuse of these words becomes evident when they are quoted by groups of Christians on opposite church corners as defence of their isolation from each other. For if each is correct, then indeed "Christ is divided" (1 Cor. 1:13)! Each may be justified in apprehending the promise to itself, but the fallacy consists in the claim that each group is together *in His name,* for His name is one of love to the brethren. "These things I command you, that ye may love one another" (John 15:17). The very faith each church seeks to proclaim is obscured and eclipsed by the lack of love which is the fruit and proof of faith.

It may be that at the present stage we should speak, not less of the unity of the Church, but more of its harmony. For the Pauline phraseology of the body of Christ implies a working together of parts, a functioning smoothly of members, by which the body itself can express a unity. Since the unifying center of the Church is Christ Himself the unity of the parts will reveal itself in their relationship to Him. All must be related to Him, but since He is one, their mutual relationships must be one of harmony if not of identity and agreement. The sin of division lies not in division, but in the strife between divisions, and the witness of self-sufficiency obstructs and obscures the witness to the sufficiency of Christ.

The only alternative which church history knows to a visible center of unity such as the papacy was the conciliar theory. There was a time in the 14th and 15th centuries when it seemed that this might be substituted for the primacy of Rome. But the affairs of church and state were so involved and motives so confused that neither before nor as a result of the Reformation did a council come to function in the name of all the churches. The great difference between this medieval movement and the present World Council of Churches lies in the freedom of the modern communions to order their affairs independently of governments. Herein lies an opportunity and the hope of an advance in the harmonious co-operation of Christian communions. Christendom will always have a variety of members of the Body of Christ—the strength and beauty of the Church depend on a variety of functions and expressions of the one body. Eliminating all divisions might mean a standardization which would leave the Church weaker and less relevant than it now is. We despair of any leadership on this earth competent to comprehend all the life of the Church. There is no possibility of a vicar of Christ or a representative hierarchy of all His fullness, in this world. For that reason the unity of the Church is eschatological. Its leadership is beyond this life, even as our citizenship is in heaven. But the witnesses to the Head of the Church are true witnesses only if they point to One Christ. And a World Council of Churches can be the witness of the Churches to a Christ whose Church is Catholic, embracing the totality and entirety of His grace.

We have spoken of the illusion of an undivided church in the Past. It is equally important that we admit the reality of a unity among all Christians in every age. For though we are prone to survey Christendom from a standpoint that reveals all its divisions, there is a point of view from which we can behold a unity unbroken by denominational boundaries. It is this substratum of unity which has made possible the ecumenical achievements of our generation.[17] It is not an accidental fact nor one peculiar to our day. For wherever baptism has incorporated men into the fellowship of faith which is the body of Christ there has existed a unity whether recognized or not. And wherever the Word has been heard and heeded there has been woven together a congregation of believers who may not know each other but are one in Christ. And wherever Christians have professed "I believe in one, holy, apostolic, catholic Church" they have witnessed to a unity given them by Christ and obscured only by their own sin and weakness. The achievement of the ecumenical endeavor is not in the creation of this underlying, unbroken, eschatological unity, but in its discovery and its insistence that this unity requires expression in the churches who confess it. Not only the ecumenical Church depends on such unity, but each and every Church exists only in the degree that it participates in the One Spirit. Paradoxically even the separated churches have their being from a unity they have not realized. When they honestly face the unity of faith across synodical or denominational lines they will have to revise even their inherited ideas on such a difficult matter as inter-communion. Personally I believe this problem will have to be attacked and solved on the parish level and in terms of individuals rather than by group action.

No one can predict the future of the present denominations of Christendom. But it is quite certain that present alignments will change. When the purpose for which certain communions were created have been served they will adapt themselves to the pressure of new events. Insofar as they are faithful to the apostolic proclamation they will be one with the Church of the Unchanging Christ, and in the measure that they appropriate the truth, the love, the holiness, of the One Christ they will find themselves in a unity with each other wherein "there can be neither Jew nor Greek, bond nor free, male and female—all are one in Christ Jesus" (Gal. 3:28).

We have seen that the tendency of the church to identify catholic with universal is not in accord with the original meaning of the word, and that therein is revealed a basic weakness in both the unity and holiness of the Church. No one local or temporal congregation is sufficient to itself. What the letter to the Hebrews says about the heroes of former generations in relation to present disciples of Christ, "apart from us they should not be made perfect" (Heb. 11:40), can be said of any communion of Christians. The perfection or fullness of Christian truth cannot be known except in a unity of Christians wherein each part contributes to the whole, and the whole is greater than any of the parts or even than the sum of all the parts. Even as the health or wholeness of the physical body depends upon the right relationship of all the members of the body to each other and their harmonious functioning, so there is a health or wholeness of the Christian Church which derives from the contribution which each member makes to the body which is greater than itself. There is an integrity of the Church which is lost when separated parts do not play their right role in the functioning of the whole. According to Colossians 3:14 the perfect bond is love, and the bond of Christ's Church is the love of Christ. There is a peace in Christ to which the Christian is called and in this peace the one body manifests itself. Not only is the bond broken when peace is destroyed by disunity, but the members of the body cannot experience in fullness nor witness in truth to the world what is the fullness of Christ. The catholicity of the Church, we said, is more than its universality, it is the love and peace which bind together all Christians and make it possible for the Church as one to comprehend the dimensions of grace. It is significant that in the same passage in which Paul speaks of the diverse ministries of the Church, he uses the language of head and body, and that this body is pictured as in the process of being "fitly framed and knit together." This happens when "every joint supplieth, according to the working in due measure of each several part" its contribution to "the increase of the body" (Eph. 4:16). We can be rightly related to the whole Christ only where we are rightly related to all other Christians. This is the essential meaning of the Church Catholic.

Christians are deficient in faith, love and hope, when they have broken the circuit which the δύναμις of Christ establishes between all who are in Him. They cannot participate in the "all in all" of Christ when they sever themselves from others in the body and think themselves in full possession of Him. One half of the Christian truth is that we are members of Christ's body, the other half is that "we are members one of another." The fourth chapter of Ephesians not only contains the great passage on the body and headship of Christ but also the passage, "Let all bitterness, and wrath, and anger, and clamor, and railing, be put away from you, with all malice: and be ye kind to one another, tenderhearted, forgiving each other, even as God also in Christ forgave you" (vv. 31-32). When we speak of the organic union of Christians we usually mean forms of organization. The organic union of which the Apostle speaks relates, it seems to me, rather to the attitude of Christians toward each other, that is, to the fellowship Christ creates among His people. Certainly present forms of denominational organization can contribute to the lack of fellowship now existing, for these are hardened barriers between Christians. But changing the organization will of itself produce no new results.[18] The fellowship of Christians is a gift of the Holy Spirit. We can grieve that Holy Spirit (v. 30) by our divisions. But it is that same Spirit who must take away our divisions and create a new fellowship. The ecumenical movement goes forward in the measure in which the churches allow the Spirit to take their thoughts off themselves and direct them to the life and work of Christ. It is the new wine of Christ's presence that we need, not new labels on old bottles.

In Ephesians 3:14-20 these facts converge in a marvelous prayer of intercession, a truly catholic prayer. It is addressed to the Father, "from whom every family in heaven and on earth is named" (every denomination!) and concludes with an ascription of praise "unto all generations for ever and ever." The apostle prays that Christians might experience "the riches of His glory," by the indwelling of Christ through faith and "being rooted and grounded in love" they might be strong (through the Spirit in the inward man) to apprehend "with all the saints what is the breadth and length and height and depth, and to know the love of Christ which passeth knowledge—filled unto all the fullness of God." The dimensions of the love of Christ can be apprehended only in a fellowship of all the saints, and the fullness of God is experienced only in a love which includes all the family of God. The unity of the Church awaits such an experience of the catholic wholeness of the Church. Catholicity pertains to a healthy, wholesome Church which a sick Church only dimly understands.

Ultimately we are not concerned only with the unity of the Church. Christ is the unity of the world. Not only the middle wall of partition separating Jew and Gentile must be moved if Christ is to realize the unity of the Church, but all the walls of partition dividing peoples, classes, generations, from each other. The New Israel is the people made one with God in the atonement of Christ, and one with each other through the ministry of reconciliation. Christ is the second Adam, with whom a new creation begins, a new race. The one new man, the unity of mankind, is the Body of Christ, a new kingdom of God into which we are "naturalized" by baptism, and in which we are held together by communion with the Present Christ. This is the plan of salvation, the divine οἰκονομια or Economy whereby God fulfills the purpose of creation. Here is a unity without which the world falls apart into meaningless and antagonistic

segments.[19] It is a breath-taking vision, too daring for the falter-
ing reason of man to follow or comprehend. But it is the apostolic message of the unity for which the Church is founded,
and in it is a catholicity of grace which constitutes all the holiness of man. "Where Christ is, there is the Catholic Church"—
the Ignatian statement still holds. Where Christ is there is the
hope of the unity of man and the world. This hope will never
reach its fruition in the aeon of time, but it is the hope which
keeps the Church alive in this time. It is eschatological, not in
the sense only that the unity of man will be realized in another
world, but in the sense that this is the "last word," the fundamental and basic word even of this world. There is no other
name given under heaven in which men and denominations can
be made one than Jesus Christ, the hope of all our glory, the
unification giving meaning to all our life.

But as we move toward the one head and center of the
Church we shall find our ways converging and ourselves closer
to brethren of other households. What form or shape the Church
may assume beyond the horizon of our present vision we cannot now describe. But what it will be depends less on what
we now conjecture about its framework and more on the spirit
with which we go forward. We ask no one to go back, nor
even to come over to our path. We ask the Spirit of God to
lead each one of us onward toward the fullness of truth and
love in Him. We believe that then barriers will crumble and
beyond present fences lies an open field where we may move
more freely as the Spirit guides us. That way lies the fulfillment of the faith expressed in our common confession, I believe
in One Holy Catholic Apostolic Church.

NOTES

[1]Martin Bucer, H. Eells (Yale, 1931); McNeill, J., *Unitive Protestantism*, (Abingdon Press, 1930). pp. 144-162.

[2]Newman, E., *Evangeliska Alliansen*, (Lund, 1937). pp. 4-7; *Dictionary National Biography;* Erich Hassinger, *Studien zu Jacobus Acontius*, Berlin, 1934.

[3]Art. by Ritschl in *Religion in Geschichte und Gegenwart*, I:1541-2; by Tschackert in *Realencyklopedie für prot. Theologie und Kirche*, III. pp. 643ff.

[4]"Molanus, Lutheran Irenicist (1633-1722)" by Samuel Miller in *Church History*, Sept. 1953, pp. 197-218. Quotation from p. 211.
Church History.

[5]J. M. Batten, *John Dury, Advocate of Christian Reunion*, (Chicago, 1944). Gunnar Westin, *Negotiations About Church Unity 1628-1634*, (Upsala, 1932).

[6]Ernest Benz, "Leibniz Und Die Wiedervereinigung Der Christlichen Kirchen," in *Zeitschrift für Religions und Geistesgeschichte 1949-50*, II Jahr. Hefte 2. pp. 97-113.

[7]The best account is a Swedish work, E. Newman, *Evangeliska Alliansen*.

[8]Newman traces it to Meldenius of Augsburg, 1612-1650, whose phrase was "In necessariis unitas, in non-necessariis libertas, in utrisque caritas," and thinks the "omnibus" came from Comenius.

[9]*Catholicity*. A Study in the Conflict of Christian Traditions in the West. —A Report presented to the Archbishop of Canterbury. Dacre Press, 1947. p. 49

[10]An interesting parallel of thought as regards the relation of the Church to the State is found in a) the section on "the Anglican Communion" in the report *Catholicity*, and b) an article by Ragnar Bring, "Stats kyrko problemet" in *Svensk Teologisk Kvartalsskrift*, 1952:2. pp. 84-105.

[11]It may be remarked that the efforts to unite the nations is almost contemporary with the movement to unite the churches—though the World Council antedates the United Nations.

[12]Those who would forget all denominations are open to Calvin's reproach against those who admit none but a perfect Church, "lest by refusing to admit the existence of a Church without absolute and sinless perfection, we should leave no Church in the World." *Institutes* II:238.

[13]*Report of the Third World Conference on Faith and Order*, Faith and Order Commission Papers, No. 15 (1952).

[14]Spener anticipated the letter of Dodd on unavowed motives by almost 300 years! *Ecumenical Review*, Vol. II, No. 1.

[15]*Pia Desideria*, Vierter Vorschlag.

[16]When the Saxons left Germany to found what became the Missouri Synod in America one of their number, Marbach, received a letter from Von Uckermann containing the hope, "May God grant you together with the firm fine faith you have—also the second heavenly gift, without which one cannot be saved—Christian love." *Zion on the Mississippi*, by Walter Foster, St. Louis, Concordia Publishing House. p. 177.

[17]William Nicholls, *Ecumenism and Catholicity*, (London, 1952) rightly calls this an eschatological event, but I cannot agree that this "ecumenical fellowship is not a theological unity" (p. 40), for it has happened only through a unity of theology unrecognized by the churches.

[18]Ernest Benz, *Bischofsamt Und Apostolische Sukzession im Deutschen Protestantismus*. Stuttgart, 1953, recalls futile attempts to create unity in German churches by "borrowing" apostolic succession.

[19]Stig Hanson, in *The Unity of the Church in the New Testament*, (Uppsala, 1946), contrasts the idea of unity in Greek philosophy in the Old and in the New Testaments.